ARTIFICIAL INTELLIGENCE IN HEALTHCARE

ARTIFICIAL INTELLIGENCE IN HEALTHCARE

Unlocking its potential

DR JANAK GUNATILLEKE

Published by N. Janak Gunatilleke, UK

First paperback edition July 2022

Book design by Henrietta Sampson
Book editing by Susan Gordon Byron

ISBN 978-1-7396374-0-8 (paperback)
ISBN 978-1-7396374-1-5 (ebook)

www.unlockaiforhealth.com

TESTIMONIALS

"This is a very welcome book that will guide clinicians, vendors, researchers, and other stakeholders about the essential steps for adopting AI in healthcare."

Dr Sandeep Reddy
Chairman, Medi-AI | Associate Professor, School of Medicine, Deakin University, Australia

"I found Janak's book to be really informative and well researched, and as a primary care clinician it gave me a much broader perspective on the use of AI in healthcare."

Dr Neil Paul
General Practitioner | Health tech entrepreneur and consultant | Digital health blogger

"A timely, well researched and accessible resource for those seeking a better understanding of the potential of AI to help address a myriad of challenges the healthcare sector in the UK is experiencing, while also providing an honest appraisal of its current limitations."

Aejaz Zahid
Director of Innovation (Integrated Care Systems)

"An excellent overview of the current AI landscape in healthcare. A must read for any stakeholder engaged in the field."

Dr Tom Oakley
Doctor | Serial entrepreneur

"A very approachable and informative book for people at all levels of expertise. Drawing on lessons from different countries to provide valuable insight for the application of AI in healthcare."

Dr Pritesh Mistry
Digital health tech innovation expert

"Packed with examples and insights from experts, this book is the go-to guide for anyone interested in how we might leverage AI to improve healthcare services and develop a healthcare system fit for the 21st century."

Dr Victoria Betton
Author | Podcaster and public speaker | Expert in human-centred design, digital strategy and adoption | Qualified social worker and coach
Dr Betton is author of Towards a Digital Health Ecology: NHS Digital Adoption through the COVID-19 Looking Glass

ABOUT THE AUTHOR

Dr Janak Gunatilleke has more than 16 years' experience in health-care. He has a specialised skill set, with experience both working as a medical doctor and developing and implementing data-driven and technology enabled improvements in healthcare. He co-founded the AI technology firm Conscient AI Labs.

Janak was a member of the evaluation panel for the NHS AI in Health and Care Award, and is a fellow of the Faculty of Clinical Informatics.

He has an Executive MBA from the University of Cambridge and is completing his dissertation for a Master's in Data Science, Technology and Innovation from the University of Edinburgh.

THANKS AND ACKNOWLEDGEMENTS

I want to thank all the people that made this book possible.

My utmost gratitude to all of those who graciously gave up their valuable time to be interviewed by me and provided me with valuable insights to make this book what it is.

Thank you to Victoria Betton, David Higgins, Tom Oakley, Sandeep Reddy, Aejaz Zahid, Mark Sendak, Charles Lowe, Neil Paul and Pritesh Mistry for their thorough reviews and very helpful feedback. Thank you to CD and Sameera, my co-founders from Conscient AI Labs, for making sure some of the technical elements were accurate.

A special thanks to Susan Gordon Byron for her excellent editing support and for Henrietta Sampson for great cover design, typesetting and layout support.

I want to thank my wife, Leah, for reviewing chapters, providing her input as a practising clinician, and most of all for her support and understanding as I worked late evenings and weekends writing. My kids provided support as only they can, giving me cuddles and making me laugh when it all got a bit too much.

CONTENTS

PREFACE

As a young boy growing up in Sri Lanka, I was always interested in technology. I remember taking my toys apart (and not always being able to put them back together!) and tinkering with electronics using a soldering iron. I was interested in understanding how things worked and started learning about computers and programming (remember BASIC and Pascal, anyone?) early on.

In the end, I didn't pursue a career in technology and instead studied medicine at university in England. After three years working as a junior doctor in the National Health Service in England, I realised that clinical medicine wasn't, perhaps, the best career for me. I wanted more variety in my work, but wasn't exactly sure what I wanted to do, so I went off to explore the world of management consulting.

Over the 14 years since leaving clinical practice, I have done a variety of things within healthcare. This includes working for blue chip and small management consulting firms, freelancing as a consultant, working in non-consulting roles, and for a health tech start-up in London. In 2017, I co-founded a niche AI consulting start-up based out of Sri Lanka. That drew me to the digital and data side of healthcare, and in 2019 I started a Master's course in data science.

I discovered two things I am really passionate about. The first is the healthcare industry, and making it better for citizens and for all those that work within the industry. My second passion? Using data and technology to help improve healthcare.

This passion for data and technology, and being part of the evaluation panel for the AI in Health and Care Awards (a multimillion-pound grant programme in England – more on this later), made me think about the wider state of AI in healthcare.

There is a lot of talk about the potential of AI in healthcare and AI is often seen as a panacea. The reality on the ground is quite different. While there are pockets of innovation in a small number of organisations, and a few exciting pilots, I couldn't think of any examples of successful large-scale, national implementations of AI in healthcare.

I began thinking about why this was. I asked myself if it was all hype or whether there was truly potential for AI to make a significant impact in healthcare. If there was potential, why were we not seeing successful adoption and scaling? What are the challenges? What could be done differently? What support do innovators and the healthcare ecosystem need?

When I started looking, I found a lot of very helpful information, with several reports and 'how to' guides available. However, I felt that most of the material was focused on a specific element, or looked at it from a specific stakeholder group's perspective. I had to 'knit together' all this for a fuller understanding. I also found that most of the content was quite theoretical, with few real life examples.

It made me want to write a book to describe my vision of a more holistic approach – taking into account key barriers, enablers, and lessons from healthcare and beyond – to improve the likelihood of successful implementation and scalability. I wanted it to be practical and to be useful to all key stakeholder groups that would be interested in AI in healthcare becoming a success. Finally, I wanted to bring in expert insights, real life experiences and to combine that with theory to bring my thinking to life.

This is that book.

It would be great to hear your feedback or to have a chat about this topic. Please feel free to reach out on LinkedIn or email me at janak@unlockaiforhealth.com

CHAPTER I

INTRODUCTION

This book describes a holistic approach to maximising the potential of AI solutions in healthcare, drawing upon academic and other published work, and practical insights and lessons learnt from industry and clinical experts. It brings together information into one place in a factual manner with supporting interviews and real life examples.

By the end of this book, you will understand more about three main areas:

- The potential of AI to add value in healthcare and to improve patient outcomes
- Where AI implementation has worked and lessons learned from where it has not
- A new approach to consider when designing, selecting and implementing AI solutions in healthcare to increase the likelihood of success and adoption at scale.

This book is aimed at:

- **Funders and policy makers** including senior management and directors within government health departments, public sector funding organisations, venture capital firms, angel investors, and central public sector health organisations, such as NHS England and Improvement (NHSE&I), including the Transformation Directorate which will incorporate the former NHSX and NHS Digital.

  You will be able to make better informed decisions on policy design and investment in the ecosystems and wider enablers (for example, data infrastructure) that will lead to more successful implementation, adoption and scaling of AI solutions. Private investors will make more informed decisions on investments and how to support those selected innovators to be more successful.

- **Buyers and operators** including staff in provider hospitals and other healthcare delivery organisations including operational and procurement managers, senior finance managers and clinicians.

  You will make better informed decisions about AI solutions on offer. You will be more confident in being involved in the co-design, on the ground implementation, monitoring and continuous improvement of these solutions.
- **Innovators and industry** including founders and senior management in start-ups and other healthcare suppliers (technology focused or otherwise).

  You will make better strategic decisions about solutions (and related functionality) to develop and invest your resources in. You will design and execute implementation strategies that avoid common pitfalls and that will result in higher rates of success and wider adoption of the solutions.

THE TIME IS NOW

AI in healthcare deserves our close attention. Let's look at the reasons why.

Healthcare systems are under enormous strain

The World Health Organisation (WHO) estimates that the percentage of the world's population over 60 years of age is due to almost double, from 12% up to 22% between 2015 and 2050, and reach a total of 2.1 billion[1]. WHO also highlights the diversity of needs among the population and the increase in certain conditions such as dementia, osteoarthritis and diabetes, as well the chances of having more than one long-term condition at the same time (multimorbidity).

A US study has shown than patients with multimorbidities have been shown to have poorer quality of life, health and physical functions, with patients with three or more conditions shown to have a significantly worse outcome that those with one or two conditions[2]. A 2018 review of 300,000 people in England revealed that of patients admitted to hospital as an emergency, the percentage who have five or more conditions increased from one in ten in 2006/7 to one in three in 2015/6[3]. It also estimated that over the five year period from 2018, patients with multimorbidities will increase total hospital activity by 14% and costs by £4 billion.

The backdrop is an increasing need to identify cost efficiencies in delivering healthcare, and often in the context of a reduction in available funding in real terms.

Covid-19 has added fuel to the fire

Covid-19 has had a significant impact across different countries on how health systems operate, elective surgical procedures, and workforces.

The waiting list for treatment on the English NHS reached 6.18 million in February 2022, a 46% increase since March 2020[4]. A review of waiting time data on elective surgeries in Finnish hospitals revealed that in 2020, compared to between 2017 and 2019, the waiting time increased on average by 8%. In certain specialities the waiting times increased up to 34%.

A US study in 2020 modelled the projected elective orthopaedic procedures (defined as total knee and hip replacements, and spinal fusions), to estimate when the health system will be back at full capacity to perform these procedures, and the size of the backlog that would have accumulated[5]. With the assumption that elective surgeries would resume in June 2020, the study estimated (in the optimistic scenario) that the health system would be at 90% of capacity after 7 months and still have more than a one million procedure backlog in two years' time in May 2022. Another US study highlighted the wider adverse effects of deferring knee replacement surgeries[6]. Apart from the continuing discomfort of osteoarthritis and inconvenience related to rescheduling surgeries, it explains that patients will suffer muscle wasting, making rehabilitation more difficult, and that it will worsen comorbidities such as depression and lead to a reduction in the overall quality of life.

The healthcare workforce was already stretched before Covid-19. WHO estimated that we will need 18 million more healthcare workers globally by 2030[7]. It is difficult to recruit healthcare workers. Despite increased demand and government plans to increase the number of general practitioners (GPs) in England, there are in fact 1,565 fewer fully qualified full-time equivalent (FTE) GPs in February 2022 than there were in 2015[8].

The American Hospital Association reports that America will have a shortage of up to 124,000 physicians by 2033[9]. There will also be shortages of other healthcare workers, especially in certain rural and urban locations. The article also highlights a survey done by the Washington Post-Kaiser Family Foundation in 2021 which showed that nearly 30% of the surveyed American healthcare workforce is considering leaving, and that nearly 60% reported an impact on their mental health from work related to the Covid-19 pandemic.

Mistakes and missed diagnoses occur during the delivery of healthcare services

A 2014 US study collated results from three studies and extrapolated the rates to the US adult population[10]. It showed a 5.08% diagnosis error rate in an outpatient setting and estimated that approximately 50% of these errors could lead to patient harm. A review of over 2,000 English primary care consultations revealed missed diagnostic opportunities in 4.3% consultations[11]. 72% of these instances had two or more contributing factors from within the processes of taking a medical history, examining the patient, or ordering, interpreting or following up on investigations. It was estimated that 37% of these instances led to moderate to severe avoidable patient harm.

A review of emergency department (ED) patient safety reports in England and Wales from 2013 to 2015 to identify diagnostic errors revealed that 86% were delayed, and that 14% were incorrect diagnoses[12]. Bone fractures were the most common diagnoses involved (44%) with myocardial infarctions (heart attacks) the second-most common (7%).

It has also been estimated that 237 million medication errors are made every year in England, leading to 1,700 patient deaths and costing the National Health Service (NHS) £98 million[13]. The highest proportion (51%) occurred during administration of the drug, with 21.3% occurring during the prescribing stage.

AI can help

AI has huge potential to add value in healthcare across a number of areas. This is across the spectrum of health, from basic biomedical sciences, drug discovery and clinical trials to the provision of healthcare services through primary and secondary care, and preventative and self-management services.

It's interesting to reflect on how AI could help healthcare professionals deliver care. The following Lynda Chin quote is included in Eric Topol's book *Deep Medicine*[14].

> Imagine if a doctor can get all the information she needs about a patient in two minutes and then spend the next 13 minutes of a 15-minute office visit talking with the patient, instead of spending 13 minutes looking for information and two minutes talking with the patient.

Studies and anecdotes from general practitioners bring to life the challenges primary care clinicians have in delivering care, often within a very short period of time, juggling to fit in several activities as well as actually talking to the patient. A systematic review of primary care physician consultation durations considering 28.5 million consultations revealed a wider range of consultation lengths, from 48 seconds in Bangladesh to 22.5 minutes in Sweden[15]. They are reported to last an average 9.2 minutes in the UK, which also needs to include arranging and/or reviewing investigations, making specialist referrals and administrative tasks to enable quality related payments[16]. The average number of problems patients present with during these consultations also differ, with 2.5 being the average in England[17] and family physicians in the US reporting managing 3 problems on average[18].

As Atul Gawande points out, the expansion of medical knowledge means that 'doctors can no longer know and do everything' and they 'must specialise in a field to absorb all the relevant information to treat a certain kind of illness'[19].

Gawande warned new doctors that[20]:

> the volume and complexity of the knowledge that we need to master has grown exponentially beyond our capacity as individuals

If AI can help healthcare professionals gather and make sense of relevant information to help them have more efficient consultations and build more meaningful relationships with their patients, that, surely, can only be a good thing.

We need to separate the hype from the reality

AI is often seen as a clever quick fix for the thorny issues related to the delivery of safe, effective and efficient healthcare.

Audiences heard Vinod Khosla, a Sun Microsystems co-founder and Silicon Valley Investor, make a controversial speech in 2012, at the Health Innovation Summit hosted by Rock Health in San Francisco[21]:

> Machines will replace 80% of doctors in a healthcare future that will be driven by entrepreneurs, not medical professionals

Predictably, Khosla's comments sparked outrage from the medical profession. I will revisit later in the book the more nuanced comments Khosla has made elsewhere, and how AI could contribute to Lynda Chin's visionary GP visit. For now, let's consider the broad outcomes. The real life results of AI in healthcare have not been impressive, and AI is nowhere near replacing 80% of doctors.

An article published by Massachusetts Institute of Technology's Review in July 2021 highlights two review papers and a report by the Turing Institute that considered the impact of AI tools developed to predict and support management of the Covid-19 pandemic[22]. The conclusions were damning. The Turing report revealed the minimal impact of AI tools; the two review papers assessed 647 tools, and concluded that none were fit for clinical use, and only two warranted further evaluation of potential.

Translation from theoretical and testing results to success in front line clinical settings can also be a challenge. The team at Google developed a Deep Learning (DL) algorithm that analysed photos of the retina (back of a patient's eye) to identify signs of diabetic retinopathy in patients in Thailand, damage caused by high blood sugar levels[23]. A successful solution could help mitigate the shortage of specialist doctors in Thailand who can review these images. The algorithm showed impressive levels of accuracy, (displaying more than 90% sensitivity and specificity, that is, confidence identifying disease and confidence when no disease identified).

The team then performed an observational study of the tool being used in the clinics covering 7,600 patients. Field work consisted of observation and interviews with nurses and camera technicians at a small selection of clinics before and following implementation of the solution. Low lighting caused issues with the quality of the images (21% of 1,838 were rejected) and could not be graded by the algorithm, which frustrated the nursing staff, who felt the image was of sufficient quality to be graded by a human specialist. Poor internet connectivity and speeds caused delays and reduced the number of patients that could be seen in a clinic (with a reduction from 200 to 100 patients screened due to a two-hour internet outage). The team is now working with the user to identify new workflows and to overcome the barriers identified.

It's not easy…

Companies applying AI to health, medicines, and biotechnology raised $12 billion funding in 2020, double the $6 billion raised in 2019[24]. However, there are a very limited number of success stories at a national scale.

The design, development and implementation of AI in healthcare is demanding. The personal and high-stakes nature of healthcare means some of the challenges common to non-healthcare settings are intensified and new, knotty problems introduced.

YOUR WAY AROUND THIS BOOK

This introductory chapter explains why it's the perfect time to fully consider AI in healthcare and provides an overview of the content I cover later in the book.

Chapter Two, *Opportunities for AI in healthcare*, identifies where AI can add value. We delve into more detail about AI and the elements relevant to healthcare. I also propose an approach to identify areas where I think AI can add value and illustrate these areas of opportunity with examples. The chapter considers the phases of healthcare delivery, and whether each is directly related to care delivery or to supporting back office functions.

Chapter Three, *Success stories*, explores successful AI implementations, both in the National Health Service (NHS) in England and in the US. I then consider large scale AI applications within the retail and entertainment industries, and identify key success factors; here are potential insights to bring back to healthcare.

In Chapter Four, *Healthcare is changing*, I delve into how the Covid-19 pandemic accelerated the adoption of digital health. I explore the key challenges healthcare was facing before the pandemic before considering how Covid-19 has redesigned healthcare and with it, and the challenges we face in the future.

In Chapter Five, *It's not easy being a machine: Trust and accountability with new technology*, I explore the background to and events shaping some of the specific challenges to AI in healthcare. Then

I identify and discuss the challenges across three areas; people, systems, and technology.

In Chapter Six, *Key themes with AI in healthcare*, I group and further reflect on the areas that are less developed, impacting the successful adoption and scaling of AI in healthcare. I illustrate some of the key themes with an example and story from IBM Watson Health.

In Chapter Seven, *Striving for good practice with AI*, I identify and discuss the key factors needed for success, and I pull in the insights and suggestions of the experts and practitioners I interviewed.

In Chapter Eight, *A roadmap for the practitioner*, I propose a holistic 3-step approach to improve the likelihood of success that incorporates the challenges, key themes and the good practices I discussed previously. I stress the importance of solving the right problem, I lay out a roadmap considering the lifecycle of AI solution development and the key stakeholder involved, and I highlight the wider enablers that are needed.

Chapter Nine, *Let's do this*, is a call to action. It is for everyone involved to work together on the approach I outline to maximise the potential of AI in healthcare.

I appreciate you may want to dip in and out of the book or want to go straight into the 'how' in Chapter Eight. Feel free to do so, because I have written each chapter so it can be read on its own.

WHAT IS ARTIFICIAL INTELLIGENCE?

There are many definitions of AI and I have seen various people use the term in different contexts, and to mean slightly different things. Before we get stuck in, I want to spend a bit of time exploring the history of the term as well as selected subsets of AI, so it is clear when I use these terms later.

In his famous 1950 paper Computing Machinery and Intelligence[25], Alan Turing asked:

> **"**
>
> Can machines think?
>
> **"**

In this paper, he described the 'imitation game' where an interrogator would try and distinguish between a human being and a computer based solely on the answers to a set of questions. This is now commonly known as the 'Turing test'. He thought that within about 50 years, computers, much like a child, could be taught, programmed to play the imitation game so well that in at least 70% of tests, most interrogators would not be able to tell the difference between the computer and a human being after five minutes of questioning.

There have been many attempts to pass the test, with constrained scenarios such as pretending to be a 13-year-old Ukrainian boy called Eugene Goostman in 2014[26] or Google's virtual assistant "Duplex" calling a hair salon and successfully booking an appointment[27], but it is generally accepted that no software has passed the Turing test in a meaningful manner. Even recent models such as GPT-3 (Generative Pre-trained Transformer), which uses deep learning to generate text similar to a human, has failed the test[28].

However, the field of artificial intelligence (AI) has made significant progress.

It is believed that John McCarthy came up with the term 'artificial intelligence' to describe the subject of a conference he organised to discuss research topics including complexity theory, neuron nets, and learning machines, in Dartmouth in 1956[29].

McCarthy put together a collection of questions and answers related to AI in 2004[30]. In this, he defines AI as:

> It is the science and engineering of making intelligent machines, especially intelligent computer programs. It is related to the similar task of using computers to understand human intelligence, but AI does not have to confine itself to methods that are biologically observable.

He also lays out the applications of AI, which include speech recognition, understanding language, computer vision to understand images and videos, classification (for example, assess customer risk when accepting credit card payments) and 'expert systems' to help users carry out tasks. (For example, the MYCIN system developed at Stanford University in the 1970s, identified bacterial infections and suggested treatments).

Machine Learning (ML) is a subset of AI which enables computers to learn through data and examples, rather than being specifically programmed with instructions. There are broadly two types of ML. Supervised learning uses a labelled dataset (where the 'correct' answer is given) to train the algorithms that are then used to make predictions. Unsupervised learning does not require labelled datasets, instead it identifies patterns itself from the dataset. Semi supervised ML sits in between, using a small, labelled dataset to learn and then apply those insights into a larger unlabelled dataset.

Deep Learning (DL) is a subset of ML, which draws inspiration from the human brain and the layered neural networks within it, allowing it to work with more large, raw and unstructured datasets to understand complex relationships in data and present more intricate insight[31].

One of the key parts of the AI 'engine' is data. To make the engine perform efficiently and accurately, the right amounts (often large quantities) of relevant and representative data is required. Furthermore, it needs to be complete, accurate and in a 'form' suitable for the AI technique being used.

CHAPTER 2

OPPORTUNITIES FOR AI IN HEALTHCARE

Although we don't yet have a full understanding of its potential, recent technological advances increase the value of AI within healthcare. It can also incrementally improve existing systems. For example, there are a large number of rules-based systems within Electronic Health Record (EHR) systems[1]. However, they can be inflexible and difficult to keep updated as medical knowledge evolves. ML based algorithms can be more accurate.

Benefits of AI for healthcare could exist in various areas, from improving health outcomes for patients, making healthcare delivery and associated administrative tasks more efficient, or even through supporting the change of healthcare delivery models.

AI is predicted to reduce healthcare costs in the US by $150m by 2026[2]. A move to a more proactive model of healthcare delivery focusing on prevention and better management of chronic diseases is expected to be a significant contributor to the reduction in costs.

However, in attempting to better understand the potential of AI, we must identify both the most promising areas (and these will evolve as the application of AI matures) and within which 'stage' of the patient journey or wider healthcare workflow there are problems to solve.

THE COMPONENTS AND AI METHODOLOGIES RELEVANT TO HEALTHCARE

AI creates opportunities for taking in and analysing large amounts of data, from different sources and in different formats. It can adapt to new situations and learn from new data. It enables the uncovering of insights, and it supports predictive analytics (what are potential outcomes?) and prescriptive analytics (what is the best action for a given scenario?).

There are several underlying AI technologies and components that are relevant to healthcare.

We discussed the high level areas of AI, ML and DL in the introductory chapter. DL enabled a step change (and generated excitement) due to the far more complex and intricate analysis it enabled.

The following are specific techniques:

Natural Language Processing (NLP)

NLP enables the processing and analysis of human language. We have not gained a full understanding of its potential to extract meaning. Its use cases include extracting unstructured data, for example, text from electronic health records (EHRs) and enabling speech recognition tools such as Alexa.

Computer vision

Computer vision enables the processing and analysis of visuals – images and videos – to extract meaning. Its use cases include image classification such as the shapes and sizes of lesions, and object detection; this would be the presence of a lesion.

Other related technologies and techniques include:

Federated learning

Federated learning enables decentralisation of the training data (for example, data to remain at individual hospitals). A central model is used by individual endpoints to train and refine the model based on local data, following which the changes and improvements are fed back to the central model while the data is retained locally, preserving privacy. The updates make the central model better, which all the individual endpoints use.

Synthetic data

To mimic real world data, synthetic data can be created by using various statistical models or by using 'generative' models (that learn from real data to be able to recreate similar data). It can help reduce data privacy issues and provide innovators access to training data, for example when there is a very limited amount of real world data.

Complementary technologies

One of the most relevant technologies within this category is robotic process automation (RPA). RPA automates repetitive tasks that use structured data. For example, copying and pasting data, opening documents or extracting structured information from systems. It is a perfect complement for AI, which can add 'meaning' to the outputs from RPA. It can also enable a staged approach to AI implementation with earlier stages focusing on RPA to deliver benefits and gain stakeholder confidence.

WHERE AND HOW AI ADDS VALUE

There is a huge and ever increasing amount of health-related data being generated each day, both by patients and wearables such as smartwatches and smartphones, and healthcare institutions and professionals in the form of medical 'records'. There are also many potentially useful data sources including social media, financial transactions and even shopping data.'

An increasing body of research and new discoveries (for example, in the fields of genomics) contributes to the extent of medical knowledge available. Covid-19 has highlighted the importance of being able to share, collate and interpret large amounts of data from disparate sources.

AI can enhance processes and outcomes from the basic sciences and research related to healthcare, related industries such as pharmaceuticals as well the core healthcare processes. In areas such as drug discovery and clinical trials[3], randomised controlled trials (RCTs) are considered the gold standard in evaluating medicines. AI can help with processing research information and real world data (RWD) as part of designing and managing RCTs more efficiently and over a shorter period of time. Pharmaceutical companies are using collaborations, for example Roche subsidiary Genentech with GNS Healthcare, to use AI to help in discovering new medicines. BenevolentAI has an AI powered platform that supports gaining insights from large amounts of data and designing target molecules to accelerate drug discovery[4]. Healx combines research, disease data and biochemical information to repurpose and improve known compounds to develop new drugs[5].

The focus of this book will be the core healthcare processes, related to healthcare systems planning, funding, delivering and monitoring health and well-being.

Areas within healthcare delivery where AI can add value can be described across three categories – non-clinical or back office, increasing productivity and enhancing delivery of care.

1. **Non-clinical or back office**

   These are activities that are not directly related to the delivery of care, but are required for the proper functioning of healthcare systems. This could include a wider range of activities from planning resource allocation, developing budgets, predicting demand (and planning capacity accordingly), checking details and making payments, and monitoring performance and compliance.

2. **Increasing productivity**

   This is an in-between category, where the activities are a mix of non-clinical, back office and direct care delivery. It could be planning of a patient pathway, or supporting a clinician to review patient notes or investigation results, or helping clinicians prioritise workload.

McKinsey Global Institute (MGI) research suggests that healthcare is one of the sectors with the lowest overall potential for automation[6]. It estimates that only 35% of time spent is suitable for automation. Considering the complex nature of healthcare and the work that healthcare professionals perform, this is not unexpected. MGI considers different healthcare occupations across Europe and further highlights differences in what can be automated. For example, medical equipment preparers (48%), medical assistants (32%) and occupational health and safety technicians (30%) perform the highest percentage of hours that can be automated. Dental hygienists (3%), orthotists and prosthetists (3%) and chiropractors (2%) have the lowest percentage of hours. General practitioners and physicians are estimated at 12%, with surgeons at 7%. Radiologists and pathologists were not analysed as a separate speciality.

The MGI research also highlights the impact, beyond considering increase or decrease in job numbers, to the change in the roles themselves. For example, the positive impact of minimising repetitive and low value administrative tasks which will enable professionals to focus on other higher value clinical activities as well as supporting the case for wider AI adoption in healthcare.

3. **Enhancing care delivery**
These are activities directly related to identifying clinical challenges and delivering (or enabling self-management of) the most appropriate interventions. AI can contribute to the interpretation of investigations, making a diagnosis, supporting a

patient to make decisions to manage their chronic diseases or optimising treatment options including medication dosages.

There are clinical specialties where there has been the most focus in the application of AI – for example, radiology. This has been driven by the baseline levels of digitisation and data available, the tech savvy nature of the healthcare workforce as well as the suitability of AI methods (for example, image analysis related) to provide highly accurate outputs.

Zhang et al developed an NLP based solution to automatically collate and categorise clinical AI research published on the Medline database[7]. An extract of the solution on 14 January 2022 from https://aiforhealth.app/ revealed 36,826 articles and the classification by clinical speciality (articles can be classified into more than one specialty) revealed the following results:

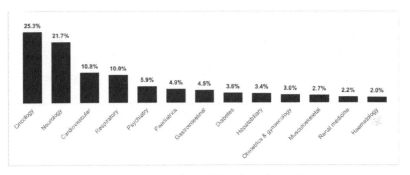

Figure 1: Research in AI by clinical specialty

The highest number of articles were published in oncology (25.3%) and neurology (21.7%), both specialities with high use of imaging used for diagnosis. Interestingly, radiology was not defined as a specialty.

A review of the US Food and Drug Administration (FDA) list of approved AI-enabled medical devices in the US, confirms radiology as the most common specialty with 70.3% of the total devices[8].

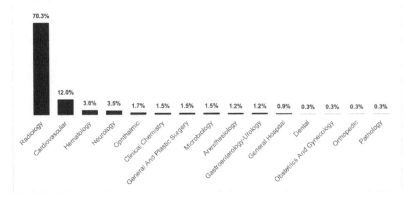

Figure 2: FDA approval of AI by clinical specialty

A review of Indian healthcare AI start-ups attracting the most investment revealed that of the top five (SigTuple, Qure.ai, Tricog, Oncostem and Niramai), at least three were focused on image analysis (Sigtuple, Qure.ai and Niarmai)[9]. Tricog has also now introduced an echocardiogram analysis solution.

The core healthcare processes begin where decisions are made and systems are put in place to promote wellbeing and deliver care to those in need, and they extend to the 'ongoing' activities related to running the health systems.

This spans across four key stages – plan, prevent, deliver, and manage.

1. **Plan**

   This stage involves preparation, review of historic data and consideration of future possibilities. Descriptive analytics, but going beyond usual data sources to consider items previously not possible without AI, will provide a solid foundation and baseline. Insights such as volumes and types of demand, capacity and resource utilisation, efficiency, and value for money (based on outcomes) will be valuable.

Planning can be at a population level, to identify the types and volumes of likely healthcare demand, as well as expected changes or trends. Second, at an operational level, the translation of these demands into actual hospital beds, activity including procedures, staff needed to support, financial commitment and other resources required. This can and should be refined across different times of the year and the type of organisation considered (such as specialist or general), and also consider scenarios including evolution of the Covid-19 pandemic to develop better resiliency. Third, the first two areas can feed into developing patient pathways that best support the population's needs, including how the supporting resources – organisations, technology and people – should be organised around the pathways.

2. **Prevent**

This stage is closely linked to the 'Plan' stage and builds on its activities to identify opportunities to be proactive. AI could enable analysis of data previously not possible and also identify insights earlier than previously.

Actions could be at a population level, for example national screening programmes for specific diseases, through to individual patient level where the actions are tailored based on individual circumstances.

Many healthcare systems, for example, England with Integrated Care Systems (ICS) – partnerships that bring together health and care organisations and budgets across a region to plan for and deliver services to meet the needs of the population – are taking a more holistic view of health. This requires wider thinking, for example considering social determinants of health, such as education, housing, work and income.

3. **Deliver**

This stage involves the spectrum of care delivery, from health-care professionals delivering care, to empowering patients to self-manage chronic conditions.

Delivery of care may start with a diagnosis, identification of a medical condition following consultation with a patient and, potentially, investigations. It could result from preventative activities, as a result of confirming a suspected diagnosis (expected 'positive' instances) of the disease or as an incidental finding (for example, a nodule on a breast screening mammogram).

The other key element is around patient interactions. This could range from helping patients find information, answering their questions, or gathering information from patients. An extension to this element is supporting patients to self-manage. This could include reminding (medications, appointments) and 'nudging' patients on healthy behaviours, to actively suggesting and making recommendations for treatment, and providing an 'escalation' route to healthcare professionals as appropriate.

4. **Manage**

Successful 'running' of health systems requires consistent quality and outcomes, efficient flow of funding and payments, value for money for goods and services procured, and a healthy and happy workforce.

Quality and outcome measures need to be clearly defined and monitored on a regular basis, with variance being flagged for appropriate action in a timely manner. Payments to providers, ideally based on outcomes rather than merely activity, need to be made following compliance checking against appropriate quality and eligibility criteria.

Supporting functions, such as finance and procurement, need to ensure that the appropriate resources, goods and services are identified, agreed, available and that appropriate payments are made in a timely manner.

Human resources departments, working alongside managers, need to ensure that the correct organisation structures are in place with suitable candidates filling the defined roles, and they are supported within a positive work environment and with the required resources to successfully perform their role.

REAL LIFE APPLICATIONS

Combining the two, 'area of activity' and 'stage of process', results in the grid view below, which provides a structured way of considering what the specific opportunities are in each scenario for AI to add value. It also provides a method of identifying example solutions or innovators developing solutions in each scenario.

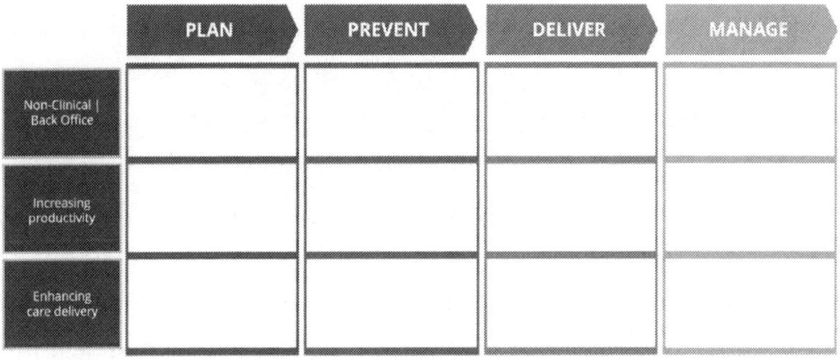

	PLAN	PREVENT	DELIVER	MANAGE
Non-Clinical | Back Office				
Increasing productivity				
Enhancing care delivery				

Figure 3: (Blank) framework to consider the potential of AI in healthcare

25

Let's consider each scenario in more detail.

Plan

Plan | Non-clinical or back office

AI can help optimise supply chain and logistics processes, ensuring the right items are in the right place at the right time. The need and opportunity was highlighted during the Covid-19 pandemic when Personal Protective Equipment (PPE) was in short supply and it was critical to get these items to those in the front line. AdviseInc developed a free solution that provided NHS hospitals an accurate single source of truth of the current stock levels and an AI powered demand forecasting element that helped better plan for the future[10].

Healthcare data is notorious for its fragmented nature and for its varied sources. Even within a single hospital data is held within different systems, for example the main EHRs, paper records, and specialist systems across clinical departments such as Picture archiving and communication systems (PACS) in radiology. This makes attempting to aggregate and analyse data difficult. Data harmonisation is the reconciliation of different data sources and related types and formats into a single 'output' that supports analysis and extraction of meaningful insights. It has been demonstrated that techniques such as ML, DL and NLP can support the collation of text data from structured and unstructured (for example, EHRs) sources and data harmonisation[11]. A related area is the use of AI to identify issues with diversity in datasets. Addressing these issues can help reduce the bias resulting from using inadequate datasets.

AI can help prioritise and allocate resources appropriately. In Brazil, DL techniques were used to develop a method of allocating financial resources across the various health regions based on public health needs[12]. A rather interesting application was the prediction of length of commitment of a healthcare worker to rural public health-care sector placements[13]. Although accuracy was low, it provides opportunities to develop these applications further and to identify interventions to improve retention, especially with shortages in healthcare workforces.

Maneesh Juneja has spent more than 20 years working with different datasets, including nine years at pharmaceutical firm GSK working with healthcare data to generate real world evidence. He is now a digital health futurist and has spent the last 10 years looking at trends in digital health and across wider society. He provides consulting services to a range of organisations around the world, helping them understand these different trends, what it means for them, and what they need to do to stay relevant.

He explains that he was in hospital recently with a family member who had just had surgery and they were trying to find a bed in the hospital for him. 'I watched the nurses frantically – for an hour – phoning different departments of the hospital to ask where a bed was available. Either they couldn't get through or they had to wait.' He says, 'These are highly qualified nurses with clinical training, right? Purely from a data perspective, why is there not a system in place that does this automatically? This must be happening all day long at every hospital in the country in the UK and in fact in many parts of the world.' We need more human doctors, more human nurses, and more beds, he says. 'If you can actually use data and you can forecast and predict in a better way, you can better allocate those finite resources.'

In March 2022, an AI powered forecasting tool developed by the NHS and AI technology firm Faculty was rolled out to 100 English hospitals[14]. It will help predict the number of admissions to EDs, enabling more efficient allocation of the healthcare workforce and beds.

AI isn't foolproof, and needs oversight. Hospitals in the US use AI based algorithms to prioritise the order in which patients with chronic kidney disease (CKD) receive kidney transplants. However, studies have shown that the models disadvantage African-American patients[15]. Removal of the 'race multiplier' (which results in higher eGFR values, a measure of how well your kidneys are working in African American patients) meant that one third would be classified as having a more severe stage of CKD (with one quarter moving up to stage 4 from stage 3B), with an impact on the optimal treatment that those patients should receive.

Plan | Increasing productivity

AI can help make operational processes in a hospital more efficient. The Judy Reitz Capacity Command Centre at Johns Hopkins University Hospital, established in 2016, is a good example[16]. Set up and run in partnership with GE Healthcare, the centre manages patient flow within the hospital and its four member hospitals. It consists of a call centre type operation, a platform collating data from across various systems including the EPIC EHR, and an AI-driven element to forecast upcoming demand.

Benefits delivered include increased bed utilisation in 2021 of 94% compared to 85% in 2016, and creating additional bed capacity, leading to an increase of $16m additional revenue per year. The centre also helped with the safe and efficient management of Covid-19 patients during the pandemic.

Another area will be the use of large datasets and machine learning techniques to extract insights supporting service design activities to develop new patient journeys. As the response to Covid-19 redesigned healthcare and changed both patient and clinical expectations, this will become an area of growing importance.

Plan | Enhancing care delivery

Neville Young is the Director of Enterprise and Innovation at the Yorkshire and Humber Academic Health Science Network (AHSN), one of 15 in England tasked with bringing innovative solutions to the NHS and helping to create economic growth. He makes an interesting point about a shift in focus in diagnosis during Covid-19. Neville explains that, previously, diagnostic companies were very keen to establish who has got what disease. This changed during the pandemic, where identifying low risk has become as important as identifying high risk so that low risk patients can be triaged more appropriately. For example, if the low risk patients on the 'two week wait' suspected cancer pathway could be accurately identified, they could be redirected appropriately (approximately 90% of the patients in this pathway don't have cancer). As well as reducing the worry for patients, it will reduce requirements along the diagnostic pathway – meaning fewer lung biopsies and CT scans.

Neville highlights a solution they are exploring in their region called PinPoint, an early cancer detection solution that uses AI to analyse blood samples taken in primary care settings[17]. PinPoint generates a score which the clinical team can then use to make a decision about the risk of cancer.

Dr Basab Bhattacharya is a consultant radiologist at Barking, Havering and Redbridge University Hospitals NHS Trust in England where he is also the joint clinical director for radiology in a department of 38 consultants and the hospital lead for AI. He explains that he got interested in AI following the publication of the NHS Long Term Plan in 2019. His interest grew further with the publication of a strategy in 2020 which outlined 'one-stop shop' Community Diagnostic hubs. AI was positioned as a solution for the increase in the workforce that would be required to staff the hubs.

In a similar vein to Neville, Basab sees the potential of AI when it has a good negative predictive value, that is, the ability to confidently rule out disease. He gives the example of an elderly patient, on blood thinning medications, who comes into the ED overnight with a head injury. In this instance a bleed into the brain needs to be ruled out. Basab explains that if the AI solution has a very good negative predictive value for blood in the head CT, then it can provide the confidence that senior ED doctors need to discharge the patient, rather than keep them overnight so a report can be reviewed in the morning.

With the explosion of healthcare, genomic and real world data, there are opportunities to develop personalised treatments and interventions. AI based methodologies could analyse large and disparate datasets to predict prognosis and identify the optimal treatments. For example, an individual's genomic information and other illnesses could result in medicine A being more appropriate and safe than medicine B.

Information about an individual's preferences, their routines, behaviours and personalities could help tailor more effective communications, getting closer to the required outcome and response. This information could be collated through real world data, as above and through a combination of historical data analysis and engagement with digital health tools. The result would be the ability to map the 'message' to the 'action by the patient'.

London based start-up DrDoctor provides a patient engagement platform with features including self-management of clinic appointments, digital clinical letters, patient assessments and video consultations. Over 10 million patients use it, with over 50 million appointments managed across 35 NHS hospitals[18]. The company is using AI to improve predictions on which patient groups (split by age and gender) are most likely to miss a clinic appointment, enabling additional reminders and personalised messages, which can be sent at the most effective time(s)[19].

Prevent

Prevent | Non-clinical or back office

A significant opportunity is monitoring and intervention to promote the health of populations. This includes identifying target populations or high risk individuals, and collecting and analysing large amounts of data to support informed decision making on regional and national interventions.

Nuria Oliver became interested in AI while at university for her undergraduate degree. Since doing her PhD, she has been focused on computationally modelling human behaviour using machine learning techniques. This is also to develop intelligent, interactive systems helpful for humans. In March 2020, and at the onset of the Covid-19 pandemic she suggested to the president of the region of Valencia in Spain, that data and AI could help enable evidence-based policy making. She was appointed by the president to lead a team of more than 20 scientists working on four areas: modelling the effects of human movement on the spread of the virus; building computational models to predict the evolution of the virus; predicting the prevalence of the disease and related hospital occupancy; finally, to develop, implement and run a large scale citizen survey to help understand citizen behaviours and impact of the pandemic on their lives. By December 2021, this had over 700,000 responses. As part of the XPRIZE Pandemic Response Challenge, which they later won, Nuria's team added a fifth area which helps evaluate public policy by weighing up social and economic costs against the benefits of reduction in the number of Covid-19 cases.

An initiative in India reviewing opportunities to improve tuberculosis (TB) outcomes used clustering (a ML technique) to identify groups of patients most likely to delay care seeking, including the specific patient factors which were driving these delays (lack of time and low perception of risk), and the 'type' of patient (employed men who drink a lot and smoke)[20]. This then enabled a more targeted intervention that could significantly reduce the spread of TB.

Prevent | Increasing productivity

AI can help make follow-ups more efficient and effective. For example, FollowApp.Care uses AI to analyse data and behavioural science to automatically engage with patients in a specific manner (personalised recalls), to promote personalised consultations and to prompt preventative actions[21]. It has been used in dental clinics to increase patient engagement (28% more completion of patient satisfaction surveys), improve patient satisfaction (52% more highly satisfied patients) and drive extra revenue (€4.2m more revenue over 7 months from new appointments from returning patients). More recently, it has also been used to automate the monitoring of Covid-19 symptoms.

Maneesh Juneja thinks personalised prevention is one way AI can add value. He explains, 'At the moment, if you see your GP, they say, hey, Maneesh you are overweight, walk more. Or they direct you to an NHS website that gives very generic advice'. He asks, 'Why can't we be using AI to give me personalised nudges, personalised reminders, personalised advice when it comes to preventing disease and improving my health? That is tailored to me as somebody of South Asian descent and who is a knowledge worker who sits all day?'

AI can predict risk and suggest interventions at both population and individual level. Specific areas of application include improving adherence to treatments and preventing admission or readmission to hospital. For example, AllazoHealth has worked with Walgreens and hospitals in North America and uses AI to identify patients at high risk of medicines non-adherence, how and what to communicate, when and how often[22].

Prevent | Enhancing care delivery

An important area is the prevention of avoidable errors and adverse effects. For example, through analysing data from EHRs, it can provide enhanced information (non-AI solutions already exist) about the risk of adverse drug reactions or interactions in order to help healthcare professionals make better decisions[23]. AI could also help predict surgical complications including post-surgical blood loss, or flag up patients at risk of developing pressure ulcers while in bed or of having a fall.

AI technology has been tested to automatically track whether patients take their medications, and correctly, including inhalers for asthma and insulin for diabetes. There is the potential to remind patients, alert healthcare professional on non-adherence, and highlight difficulties they may have using the medications[24].

Neville Young highlights a use case where AI could help engage and diagnose those patients who attend fewer appointments, by providing them with the ability to perform simple self-testing at home. He provides the example of healthy.io, which uses AI to help analyse urine samples in a patient's home using their smartphone and a test kit[25]. It can determine the ACR (albumin to creatinine ratio) in the urine to help with early diagnosis of chronic kidney disease. Neville explains this can help health workers to engage with all patients and in particular, and with the right engagement, those from more socioeconomically deprived areas, who traditionally might not have engaged well with the healthcare system, therefore helping address the associated health inequalities.

Jvion uses AI to analyse various clinical, socioeconomic and behavioural data to identify patients with hidden risk factors that are more likely to be readmitted to hospital and recommends personalised interventions[26]. A study of an implementation of a Jvion solution at a regional hospital in Wisconsin demonstrated a 25% relative reduction in the risk of readmission through recommendations including arranging specific post-discharge referrals, implementation of specific management plans (for example, weight or pain management) and extra patient education[27].

Deliver

Deliver | Non-clinical or back office

AI can support the more efficient delivery and support of healthcare services. General opportunities include day-to-day running of clinics and hospitals such as scheduling of appointments.

Specific opportunities will differ based on the health system. In the US, physicians reported an increasing burden with prior authorisations, and healthcare executives identified it as the area with most potential for AI application[28]. Prior authorisations require understanding details about the patient's health care plan, identifying which services and medication require prior authorisation and collecting documentation for approval. Infinx has an AI powered solution that works with EHRs[29].

Deliver | Increasing productivity

AI can support healthcare professionals and the wider workforce in the delivery of healthcare.

It can help healthcare professionals during procedures. For example, a real time polyp (small growths) detection system with visual and auditory cues during colonoscopy increased the adenoma detection rate by 43%[30]. This was due to an increase in the number of smaller sized polyps that were detected. As well as enhancing the performance of experienced doctors, this type of feedback can also be useful to support the training of junior doctors.

AI can also help reduce healthcare professional workloads. Amazon's Alexa has been deployed in some areas as a virtual assistant into hospital rooms, where it helped patients with simple tasks such as changing the channel on the TV and calling the nurse for help getting out of bed[31]. Eunpyeong St. Mary's Hospital in Korea uses robots, named 'Robot Paul' and 'Robot Maria', equipped with abilities such as self-driving, to support medical staff on ward rounds (that is 'Robot Paul') and to guide patients and visitors around the hospital and to their scheduled appointments (that is 'Maria'). Robot Paul provides information to medical staff including inpatient lists and clinical information from the EHR for specific patients, and also transcribes speech into text to transcribe notes back into the EHR.

Reducing administration and non-clinical workloads could help colleagues spend more time on developing meaningful doctor-patient relationships, and as described by Topol move from 'shallow medicine' to 'deep medicine', making 'healthcare human again'[32].

Another example, at the University of Pennsylvania, a chatbot named 'Penny' uses AI to help improve medication adherence, reduce calls to the hospital and reduce visits to the ED[33].

Deliver | Enhancing care delivery

AI can support the diagnosis of medical conditions, provision of healthcare services and help patients self-manage chronic conditions like diabetes and heart disease.

Yosef Safi Harb really enjoyed maths and physics at school, and progressed to aerospace engineering and mechatronics. However, in the aerospace and automobile industries, he felt the impact of the work was limited. There is a lot to do in healthcare, using sensor knowledge to provide good quality care using this portable technology. After meeting some cardiologists with similar interests, the idea for Happitech was hatched. Happitech allows people to use their smartphone camera and PhotoPlethysmoGraphy (PPG) to measure blood flow based on light level reflected in the blood to screen patients for atrial fibrillation ('irregularly irregular' heartbeat which increases the risk of conditions such as strokes). By choosing the right risk populations – over 75 years of age, with comorbidities, etc. – it can enable cost effective screening compared to population-wide screening.

Wysa, which provides cognitive behavioural therapy (CBT) techniques provided through a chatbot, supports individuals dealing with mental health challenges[34]. Emma Selby is a mental health nurse by background, with experience working with child and adolescent mental health services, and she is currently the clinical lead at Wysa. She got involved in technology in 2014, while doing a postgraduate degree in improving access to mental health. Emma was working with young people, mainly 14-15 year old, who hardly ever called and mostly sent text messages. They told her how the system wasn't working for them, especially having to call to make appointments and talk on the phone. They told her how much extra stress this was putting on them and how anxious it made them feel. Emma started to explore how apps and technology could help, and found an article about Wysa.

Most of the other tools still relied on a human at one end. Emma explained that the majority of teenagers presented to the ED between 10pm and 2am, meaning a solution that wasn't manned out of hours wasn't going to be very helpful. Through her work, Emma realised that they didn't always need a clinician on the other side of the keyboard and that what the patients needed was the clinical information that was given to them, which was often the same for the same scenario and patient. Emma observes that her explanation of mindfulness doesn't really change depending on who she described it to. She was thinking, 'Why can't this be automated?' and 'Surely we can do a better job than a YouTube video? We can then check what they actually practice.' Emma says that the Wysa solution not only improves the user journey, but also removes a huge amount of clinical administration and can help reduce waiting lists that might be several months long. It also allows monitoring of progress and early identification of any deterioration while patients are on the waiting list.

The Madrid-based start-up ifeel is a workplace wellbeing platform with over 400,000 users, providing both access to sessions with psychologists and self-care tools such as daily mood trackers, exercises and supporting content. It uses AI to recommend the most relevant exercise and content to users[35].

When deployed through chatbots such as Babylon and Ada, AI can also support patients in working through their symptoms, suggesting diagnoses and generating a self-care treatment recommendation or that the user seek further input from a healthcare professional where appropriate.

Manage

Manage | Non-clinical or back office

Important supporting functions during this stage include making accurate and appropriate payments to providers in a timely manner. In countries with mainly private healthcare systems such as the US, this means reviewing and processing insurance claims. In countries with public healthcare systems, like the UK, this could involve assessing providers against agreed performance and quality criteria.

US based technology firm Olive AI has developed an AI platform which incorporates automation functionality to provide payers with a 'clearinghouse' solution which supports the processing of claims[36]. The solution can edit claims in real time, increasing accuracy in an effective manner, keeps providers updated on claim and payment status, answers questions from payers on eligibility and maintains information on claims and payment details. Olive AI also provides equivalent solutions for providers, to support them with checking claim status, accurate resubmission of denied claims and prioritisation of payments due[37].

Alex Kafetz is the Head of International Strategy and BD at Beamtree[38] in Australia, an ASX listed company. Its CEO is Tim Kelsey, founder of Dr Foster, which pioneered the publication of patient outcomes and risk adjusted mortality rates across the NHS. Beamtree makes it simple for healthcare providers to access quality information, to automate wherever possible and make informed decisions.

He believes that if AI can help automate routine administrative work then that means that the clinicians and other healthcare staff can spend more time with the patient. One key innovation being pioneered at Beamtree is computer assisted clinical coding. Alex explains that, in Australia, the company analyses data quality for approximately 90% of the hospital episodes each night and feeds it back to the hospitals. They are now partnering with a number of NHS hospitals[39] where Alex thinks they can use pattern recognition and machine learning to automatically code the majority of patient records overnight after discharge. That means the coders can then be more usefully deployed in coding the remaining cohort which is quite complex, and intellectually stimulating.

Apart from the increase in efficiency, Alex explains that there are additional opportunities where the AI based solution can provide value. By using AI to more accurately code each admission to include all the procedures and interventions received (Alex estimates a 16% error rate in England), the hospital can ensure it will get the full reimbursement from the payers. Further, by using AI to consider combinations of diseases and diagnoses that typically occur together, it can flag up expected or less likely diagnoses that would be expected. Finally, AI can be used to identify potential issues or coding omissions – for example, where a patient diagnosed as having diabetes five years ago does not have a coded diagnosis for diabetes for this admission. With better quality data capture, the information is better standardised and is more useful for planning and research or benchmarking.

Alex also points out the solution is not to put coders 'out of business', but to fill the gap, because there are not enough coders to do what is required.

AI can also support performance monitoring and audits more efficiently through enabling targeted sampling. In Zambia a pilot verifies performance-based financing through the use of ML techniques such as Naive Bayes, Logistic Regression and Random Forests to audit 11% of the population across two features – financial payments and equipment upgrades[40]. Random Forests performed the best, suggesting a cost effective and feasible approach to verifying payments in this environment.

Manage | Increasing productivity

AI can reduce the burden on healthcare professionals by effectively engaging with patients and support them in reviewing and improving their practice.

Yokeru is an automated calling technology that can call sheltered housing tenants on their mobiles or landlines to check they are okay and to gather further information through surveys. It can increase the reliability of the tenant being called on time and saves sheltered living scheme managers time, and notes which calls were made[41]. If the tenant indicates they are not well or doesn't pick up the call, it gets escalated automatically.

AI can help extract data and insights from medical notes, for example using NLP. This can enable review of specific patients and their management, which can be used for continual development of healthcare professionals. This in turn can foster learning health systems, where a culture of continual improvement is prevalent, best practice and data generation is embedded into delivery processes and knowledge gained through data is used to improve practice[42].

Dr Tom Foley studied software engineering and economics before moving to medicine and becoming a consultant child and adolescent psychiatrist. He is also the Principal Investigator on the Learning Healthcare Project, a Health Foundation-funded study aiming to explore the meaning, feasibility and implications of the Learning Health System concept. Foley highlights that although people think data saves lives, it doesn't. Knowledge applied at the front line, at the point of decision is what saves lives. A 'learning health system' is basically the evolution of an ordinary health system, he says, towards one that learns from every patient who is treated, and is technology and data enabled.

Dr Basab Bhattacharya points to another application of NLP in helping coordinate care and follow ups. He gives the example of where a patient has an investigation such as a CT scan and has a report, but the result is not made available or the right 'alert' is not shared with the relevant clinician to take action on a timely basis. It can also be useful to automate follow ups and admin tasks to ensure activities in a defined clinical pathway (for example, a follow up appointment in two weeks) are not missed.

Manage | Enhancing care delivery

AI can support the delivery of care remotely and monitoring of patients in their homes.

Eko has developed advanced stethoscopes and combined ECG devices with increased accuracy, and supported by AI-driven analysis[43]. They are designed to be suitable for telehealth scenarios and for use in patient's homes.

Huma has a remote monitoring platform which connects patients and healthcare professionals, and provides care plans, questionnaires and patient education, and functionality for device integration and for patients to capture vital signs[44]. It provides healthcare professionals with real time views of their patients and identifies patients at risk. During Covid-19, the company used data from 11,245 participants testing positive for Covid-19 to develop and validate a machine learning model, which identified new predictors for mortality and which can be useful in personalised risk profiling and monitoring of disease progression[45].

Putting it all together

Fitting the examples above into the framework introduced in Figure 3 provides a structured view of the areas and stages AI can add value in healthcare.

	PLAN	PREVENT	DELIVER	MANAGE
Non-Clinical | Back Office	• Supply chain and logistics optimisation • Health data collation and harmonisation • Resource allocation	• Population health • Identifying target patient groups for specific interventions	• Optimising the supporting functions such as finance and HR • Optimising routine/admin tasks such as scheduling	• Enabling accurate and timely payments • Supporting more efficient auditing
Increasing productivity	• Managing patient flow in a hospital • Designing new patient pathways	• Optimising patient follow ups • Running campaigns to provide personalised interventions	• Enhancing human-led procedures • Reduce workload and demand on healthcare professionals	• Supporting care delivery and automating processes • Extracting information from EHRs to support continuous improvement
Enhancing care delivery	• Identifying personalised treatment • Planning personalised patient communications	• Identifying high risk groups • Prevent avoidable errors and adverse drug effects	• Enhancing investigations and diagnosis of disease • Supporting self management • Supporting triage	• Solutions to support remote monitoring • Solutions to support remote care delivery

Figure 4: (Completed) framework to consider the potential of AI in healthcare

The scaling of adoption of AI in healthcare will be an evolution and the above grid approach helps identify the most obvious initial target areas, for example non-clinical or back office, as well as certain specialities such as imaging and pathology. Successful implementation of solutions for these use cases will build confidence, momentum, and develop enablers needed to move on to more challenging use cases.

CHAPTER 3

SUCCESS STORIES

The potential of AI has been realised in real life, in healthcare and other industries, but in certain industries and applications, for example in entertainment and e-commerce, the scale of adoption and impact has been far greater and more consistent.

Babylon provides online consultation services and AI powered solutions such as symptom checkers. Despite divided opinions on the accuracy of its AI, and the far from universal acceptance of its positioning and approach to implementation within the NHS, it has achieved impressive scale globally.

Driven by aggressive growth in the US, Babylon announced that it expects its January 2022 revenue to be $80m, increasing its full year 2022 projection to $900m – $1bn, a three-fold increase over 2021 revenue[1]. The increase equates to a significant CAGR (Compound Annual Growth Rate is the 'average' growth each year within that period, calculated in a compound manner considering both the original amount and the growth amount) of more than two-fold over the last 4 years. Ali Parsa, CEO of Babylon, positions its trajectory alongside the biggest players in retail and hospitality:

> While our continued growth may seem extraordinary in the healthcare universe, it is not unlike the levels of the many well-known disruptive digital innovators such as Amazon, Netflix, Tesla, or Airbnb, who also experienced similar growth in their 'take-off' years

Babylon compares its 4 year CAGR (230%) to those Netflix (74%), Amazon (59%), Airbnb (146%) and Tesla (126%). Even though revenue does not equal impact – it is not a direct comparison of the same actual years across the companies are different, and the proportion of revenues driven by AI is different (for example, a high percentage for Babylon versus an expected lower percentage for Tesla) – it is still interesting to see Babylon's growth in the context of other innovators that have had a huge impact on day to day lives.

AI IN HEALTHCARE

There have been successes in using AI in healthcare across different use cases. It is useful to review the details in order to gain a better understanding of key success factors.

Improving the delivery of Covid-19 related care

Dr Rizwan Malik is a Consultant Radiologist and Divisional Medical Director for the Diagnostics and Support Services Division at the Royal Bolton Hospital in England. He has always had a strong interest in AI. Rizwan pioneered the successful use of Qure.ai's qXR solution as part of Royal Bolton's Covid-19 response. The solution was originally developed to detect tuberculosis and has a CE certification for that use case.

Qure.ai came to Rizwan's attention when he was thinking of a way to trial the use of AI safely without impacting patient care directly, and was proposing a use case of report quality assessment using AI. When the pandemic hit, the company rapidly redeveloped qXR to detect Covid-19.

qXR is now a standard part of the chest x-ray (CXR) analysis workflow in the trust, providing clinical decision support. It delivers a number of benefits. Firstly, qXR provides clinicians with a quick view at the time of performing CXR regarding the risk of Covid-19 and the percentage of the lung involved, which enables timely decisions to be made around the need for intensive care and when to safely step down care. It serves as a clinical decision support system, like a valuable member of the team.

It supports trainee radiologists and acts as a quality check. Importantly, it provides improved support and confidence in CXR interpretation by junior doctors. Rizwan recalls that this was actually the first benefit relayed back to him by the hospital's clinicians – how much better their juniors were at reviewing CXRs with this support.

Rizwan also finds it speeds up and streamlines patient flow in the ED and in wards by helping in triage and giving 24/7 clinical decision support, reducing the mean turnaround time for image interpretation from five days to three minutes.

Several factors contributed to the successful adoption of the qXR solution[2,3].

According to Dr Hugh Harvey, another radiologist and AI expert, Qure.ai has put a lot of effort into identifying and answering a real problem.

At the hospital, Rizwan was part of establishing a Digital Innovation Board, which included the chief information officer, medical director and other radiologists, to discuss AI offerings from companies. It was a mechanism to bring internal stakeholders together in the trust to explore the concept of using AI. What started out as a talking shop about the art of the possible provided access to already-engaged stakeholders across IT, finance, and information governance (IG) when it came to considering a use case in earnest.

The company had a clear view on the training data (and its applicability to the patient population in question), data governance (including who owns the data and who benefits commercially) and data security. Rizwan explains that the trust also chose to have a server installed by Qure.ai behind the trust's firewall as an added IG precaution, and to prevent any patient identifiable data leaving the trust.

The solution was positioned to support clinicians but with those doctors retaining both responsibility for the diagnosis and the ability to override the solution where appropriate. This enabled acceptance and adoption from the doctors.

Enhanced the outcomes for stroke patients

We saw AI helped with Covid-19 patients, but what about examples where it has improved the delivery of care for other widespread and serious diseases?

The Royal Berkshire NHS Foundation Trust in England sees around 700 patients with stroke each year. Its 24/7 acute stroke service thrombolyses – that is, it dissolves the clot – in 20-25% of the admitted patient[4]. The thrombolysis service was delivered by doctors working on a rota and patients were reviewed in person in the ED. If thrombectomy (the mechanical removal of the clot using a catheter passed via the blood vessels) was deemed necessary, patients had to be transferred to a specialist hospital.

There were several challenges affecting how the service operated. Decisions to thrombolyse or refer for mechanical thrombectomy rely on ED doctors who may have differing levels of clinical experience and confidence in the field, and fewer resources to call on out of hours. There were inconsistencies in how the thrombolysis rota was staffed, based on the time of the day and day of the week. Additionally, brain imaging was only available via hospital computers, so it was difficult to provide consistent access to specialist reviews, for example, when the consultant was not at the hospital.

Dr Kiruba Nagaratnam is a consultant stroke physician, geriatrician, and the clinical lead for stroke at the hospital. He became interested in streamlining the stroke pathway.

Kiruba explains that the local hospital doesn't have a thrombectomy service and therefore needed to send patients requiring thrombectomy to either Oxford or London. They were struggling to get timely reports on CT Angiograms, a special type of CT scan where contrast dye is injected into the patient to enhance the image. Kiruba remembers that it could take up to two and a half hours to make the diagnosis and refer the patient, by which point some patients may no longer be clinically suitable to receive the treatment.

During Covid-19, he worked with colleagues to incorporate the e-Stroke solution by Brainomix, a UK-based AI company, into the hyper-acute stroke pathway at the hospital. It uses machine learning techniques to review CT scans of the brain to identify and quantify ischaemic damage, and identify blockages of blood vessels in the brain. Work with Brainomix started before Covid-19, in 2019, and it took almost a year to finalise IG and other approval processes. When e-Stroke went live in March 2020, Kiruba thought 'We have got this solution that really works, how can we make the best use of it in the context of Covid-19?'

The hospital accelerated the adoption of e-Stroke's cloud capability, supporting the use of a linked smartphone app. The app allowed the on-call stroke or neurology consultant to view the images (along with AI driven decision support as above) wherever they were. It also enabled the sharing of pseudo-anonymised images outside of the hospital, to enhance the referral process or to seek expert opinions.

This AI enhanced pathway delivers several benefits. Consultants who are self-isolating due to Covid-19, or working remotely for other reasons, can still support the pathway. ED doctor time, previously taken up by the stroke pathway, has been freed up, allowing ED doctors to focus on other clinical care. It also enabled specialist stroke and neurology consultant cover during weekends. Finally, instant access to images reduced delays to treatment, and the ability to share pseudo-anonymised images improved the quality of referrals to specialist centres.

Kiruba highlights three key success factors. The existing organisational culture was very pro-innovation and pro-digital, and willing to try out new solutions if it was going to create value for patients. The collaboration identified a well defined need, then found a solution to address the problem; it was not 'going to a conference, seeing an AI solution and then trying to bring it back and shoehorn it into a problem that never existed'. The third factor was the relationship the hospital developed with Brainomix, adopting a partnership approach rather than transactional client-supplier interactions.

Kiruba explains that e-Stroke software makes the overall process – how fast they make the diagnosis and the referral – more efficient by speeding up decisions, and therefore other elements of the pathway, and the people involved are motivated to complete tasks faster.

Dr Basab Bhattacharya also implemented e-Stroke at his hospital. One of the measures he used in this instance was time to make a management decision. Basab explains that while it was 'not a perfect solution', it allowed the time to be reduced by 75%.

A key element Basab considers is cost. He highlights an interesting measure he uses to assess cost: units of Healthcare Assistant (HCA) wages, which is approximately £20,000 per year. 'The number of avoidable deaths you see through things like elderly people not being fed correctly, not being washed correctly, and so you've got to look at what boring things you can do with the money.' He says that getting more radiologists was not viable, and Brainomix was cost effective.

Kiruba says they are in the process of developing an academic paper for peer-reviewed publication. It was presented at the International Stroke Conference as an abstract, and demonstrates that the functional outcomes for patients have improved significantly.

Making it safe for patients who have severe infections[5,6]

Looking beyond the NHS in England are other success stories, AI technology developed in a different healthcare system and with different ways of working.

Dr Mark Sendak is the Population Health and Data Science Lead at the Duke Institute for Health Innovation. First a mathematics student, he later studied medicine and policy, working with healthcare organisations and clinicians to make the best use of health data.

Duke University Hospitals (DUH) first tried to implement a sepsis detection system in 2015 based on triggering a best practice advisory (BPA) if the National Early Warning Score (NEWS) was 7 or higher[7]. The nurse had to click a button to record that the rapid response team (RRT) had been called or specify why they hadn't been called (for example, if the patient was already known to have sepsis). The performance of the system was poor, (interestingly it performed worst during the 48 hours following admission, when most events occurred), and didn't have a significant impact on patient outcomes. One of the reasons for failure was the excessive number of alerts it generated – more than 100 times a day for some high risk patients – leading to 86% of alerts being ignored by the clinicians.

SEP-1 was a tool which measures compliance with the Centers for Medicare and Medicaid Services (CMS) 3-hour and 6-hour treatment bundles for sepsis. In 2016, DUH performance on SEP-1 was poor. SEP-1 results were also due to be published publicly soon.

Sepsis Watch is a machine learning-based sepsis detection and management solution that uses information from the EHR to predict the sepsis risk of patients presenting to the ED. It began with project work in 2016. The ED was chosen as the area of focus as analysis revealed most cases of sepsis occurred within 24 hours of presentation to the ED. Mark explains that AI can help 'shift the locus of intervention upstream'. Sepsis was mainly managed in the Intensive Care Unit (ICU) or on inpatient wards. 'Where is the actual point of entry?' Mark asks, 'that's where you need to intervene'. Sepsis Watch uses a web application that's accessible from any web-enabled device, which is monitored regularly by a nurse (they primarily use iPads), to alert the user to patients who are at high risk. The nurse can review the information and if appropriate, call the ED physician to confirm the diagnosis and place orders for treatment.

Mark explains that the primary objective was to improve the hospital's compliance with the sepsis bundle best practices. Before Sepsis Watch, DUH's compliance was 31% and after the first year it doubled to 64% [8]. Mortality appears to have also decreased, although a final evaluation of the solution is not yet finalised.

There were several factors that contributed to the success of the project, which began initially as a 12-month pilot.

Taking on board lessons learned from the first project, the Sepsis Watch team focused on reducing alarm fatigue by having a nurse screen the alerts and only call a physician where they felt a sepsis diagnosis was likely and needed to be confirmed. Working with clinicians, it was determined that up to four high risk alerts per hour for a single RRT nurse was ideal, and 50 high risk cases were reviewed to develop the optimal alert thresholds.

The project utilised a multidisciplinary team consisting of clinicians, machine learning experts and a full-time innovation team working together to design, develop and implement the solution. This enabled deep understanding of the problem and a solution that integrated with existing ED clinical processes and workflows.

The Sepsis Watch team developed trust in meetings and information sessions with communication of both quantitative information such as model performance and qualitative information such as patient stories. This built on the focused engagement carried out in the four weeks leading up to go-live.

The team developed an 'enterprise' solution integrating with the hospital EHR system, tested to manage required activity volumes and security aspects, backed up by a responsive support function.

A governance committee was created, consisting of clinical and administrative stakeholders, to promote the new technology, provide training and communication, develop metrics, and monitor effectiveness, and plan for the long term sustainability of Sepsis Watch.

Mark confirms this was the first deep learning model put into an operational health setting in the US.

BEYOND HEALTHCARE

To better understand the opportunities for AI in healthcare, it is helpful to consider where AI has been successfully deployed in day to day life and across other industries.

AI systems are embedded in products and technologies commonly used by almost everyone. Speech recognition technology is prevalent in everyday life with the popularity of Apple Siri, Amazon Alexa, and Google Assistant. Microsoft made a significant play into this area in healthcare with the acquisition of Nuance (who developed the Dragon dictation software) in 2021. Apple FaceID and Windows Hello use Computer Vision technology to provide facial recognition functionality to secure laptops and mobile phones. Following Covid-19, Apple even improved FaceID to support recognition when users are wearing face masks.

Platforms such as Facebook and Twitter use machine learning to optimise what content users see and to help moderate content. Credit card companies have been using machine learning techniques to improve accuracy and prevent 'false alarms' when detecting fraudulent activities and alerting customers.

McKinsey's Global Survey of AI in 2021 revealed that 56% of organisations reported AI adoption in at least one function, up from 50% the year before[9]. It also highlighted that 27% of respondents attributed at least 5% of earnings before interest and taxes (EBIT) attributable to AI (up from 22% the year before). There was a stronger impact on cost savings, with respondents reporting higher cost savings across all functions compared to the previous year.

Why does AI's prevalence vary so much between industries?

Thinking about products we interact with in our everyday lives, you have probably already concluded there are many more examples of success in other industries than there are in healthcare.

Chalinda Abeykoon is passionate about entrepreneurship and believes that it can be an ethical way of empowering people and providing them with financial independence. He has been involved in launching first of type government-funded incubators and accelerators in Sri Lanka, and in raising the first micro-VC fund in Sri Lanka. Along the way, he has mentored over 3,000 entrepreneurs and helped build 50 start-ups. Over the last couple of years, he has also worked across South and Southeast Asia.

Chalinda explains that AI is higher up in the value chain and that one of the key predictors of adoption of AI into a specific industry is how much technology is already adopted by the industry. In a context where some of the 'core' systems such as EHRs and appointment systems are not present, trying to sell an AI solution in healthcare is going to be very hard. Chalinda notes that where AI is really delivering benefits is in environments where technology is already prevalent, for example Netflix.

In most cases where companies adopted AI solutions actively, data was available readily and in large quantities that enabled development and refinement of effective AI models. The examples we will discuss shortly have more than 100 million users each, providing a large and rich data source. Additionally, the data was available regularly or even in real time, and covers a range of elements that provide rich insights into user behaviours and preferences.

Since most of the data used by these large companies came from a single or small number of sources, controlled mainly by the company itself, the data was structured in a standardised manner, making collation and analysis easier. The companies also have sophisticated methods to monitor for anomalies in the vast amounts of data to ensure a good quality across the datasets[10]. For example, Uber has a platform called the Data Quality Monitor (DQM) that uses various statistical modelling techniques to automatically monitor the numerous datasets, also predicting any potential errors that may occur next. It also created a scoring system (0 to 4, with 4 being very anomalous) to alert data owners. Amazon automates data validation and focuses on Application Programming Interfaces (APIs) that allows users to define checks and constraints on the form of the data.

In each instance, they were solving a real problem (for example, how to make warehouse operations more efficient at scale) or aiming for a clear goal to add value to the customer, (such as finding the most efficient route in traffic saving time and money).

Furthermore, models used by these successful companies were never built in isolation or as an afterthought, but rather have been embedded seamlessly into products and user journeys For example, FaceID allows users to secure their iPhone without the hassle of having to remember or enter passcodes.

In the retail and entertainment industries, there are fewer consequences to bias in algorithms with respect to race or gender: if the accuracy of a book or film recommendation on Amazon isn't perfect, the customer may not take action, but there is no harm done.

Maneesh Juneja thinks there is an opportunity for the healthcare industry to look at what industry has done and 'hyper personalise' the communication between the system and the patient. Rather than generic health advice for an entire population, learn from how other sectors have used data to tailor messaging and improve engagement.

There are opportunities to be more specific with messages and to optimise human responses, especially where generic communications may not be encouraging patients to engage or comply with medical advice.

Of course, behavioural change theory explains that hyper-personalisation of messaging, in itself, will not lead to people changing their health behaviours. Other complementary factors need to be taken into account. For example, studies have demonstrated that expectancy priming (flagging whether the message they receive in an individualised one or a standard one), autonomy support (using language that were less directive and encouraged people to consider their choices) and exemplar messaging (providing reference role models for the behaviour) can increase the individuals belief in their capacity to do what's required to make the behaviour change[11].

There are several underlying factors enabling the widespread adoption of various AI solutions, especially in retail and entertainment. To better understand the impact of AI, it is useful to consider how it is applied at commercial powerhouses Netflix, Amazon and Uber.

AI operating at scale

Several companies have deployed AI at a significant scale to enhance the customer experience, and, as a result, brand revenues and reputation. To illustrate the points, it is worth spending some time with these brief case studies, bearing in mind the differences highlighted in the section above, for three examples of AI success stories in retail and entertainment.

Netflix

Netflix's founders have almost always been using data to understand its customers better, starting with collating information gathered from user surveys and phone calls. As early as 2012, Mohammad Sabah, then a senior data scientist at Netflix, observed that the company captured and analysed a huge amount of data to predict what users would like to watch next[12]. Even then, 75% of users chose movies based on automated recommendations.

Netflix is using AI in several ways to improve customer service.

It supplements the creative and more traditional 'showbiz' criteria of deciding which shows to commission with insights derived from data. It uses transfer learning (models trained for one task before being used on another task) to help answer the following questions more effectively and at scale for a potential new show, 'Which existing titles are comparable and in what ways?' and 'What audience size can we expect and in which regions?'[13]. The success rate for Netflix original shows is reported to be 80% when the industry standard is 30-40%[14].

Netflix uses AI to personalise the shows it recommends to users, based on their previous viewing history and that of others with similar tastes. It gathers ratings through a rather non-traditional 'thumbs up or thumbs down' system, and not the more traditional 1 to 5 rating scales. It also presents a 'percentage match score', which is how probable the streamer thinks a specific user is likely to like (and give a 'thumbs up' to) that show. A paper published by a Netflix team in 2015 estimates that the personalisation and the recommendation system saves the company $1bn a year[15]. The company also uses AI to personalise the thumbnails of the shows for specific users, by changing the image that is displayed.

Netflix also uses AI to make operations more effective. For example, it optimises video streaming using compression to meet varying internet bandwidths of users across different geographies, alongside an automated quality control system to help identify audio, video and text that needs to be improved.

Netflix had 222 million subscribers worldwide in January 2022, although the growth in subscriber numbers in 2021 was the lowest since

2015 and stood at only 50% of the (pandemic fuelled) growth seen in 2020[16]. Netflix reported revenue of $28.63bn in 2021, up 14.56% from the $24.99bn in 2020[17]. It is also facing stiff competition; Disney, for example, now has 179 million subscribers across its platforms.

Amazon

The company was an early adopter of AI, sharing data across internal departments and developing a business strategy to maximise their competitive advantage[18]. Amazon's approach to AI has been described as a 'flywheel'. Following the initial substantial effort to get the wheel spinning in the first place, a coordinated effort across departments working on and using AI outputs means that lower and sustainable amounts of effort can enable continual benefits for the whole organisation.

Amazon is using AI to improve the service it offers its customers and make its operations more efficient. Firstly, it powers the recommendation functionality that suggests products for users based on their browsing history, previous purchases and considering similar items bought by other users. It has developed the Amazon Personalise tool that supports developing recommender system solutions and a proprietary algorithm (A9, recently updated to A10) to make recommendations more relevant[19]. Personalised product recommendations increase site traffic, user engagement and satisfaction, and sales. A McKinsey analysis estimated that even in 2013, AI-generated product recommendations accounted for 35% of sales[20].

AI is used within the search functionality to improve the accuracy and usefulness of the results that are generated. One use case is to improve the matches for a customer query by understanding the context[21]. Amazon researchers explain that a neural network based model is used to predict the context of use – for example, predicting the customer is interested in 'running' when they search for 'adidas men's pants'. 81% of human reviewers agreed with the 'context' chosen by the system.

AI is also part of Amazon's warehousing and logistics operations. Typical fulfilment centres are 600,000 to one million square feet in size with one to four million products bins[22]. The company uses computer vision systems to identify where items are and for robots to work alongside with humans. AI helps predict demand to help identify what to sort and where to place it (closest to customers who will buy it), and to reduce incorrect sorting of products. Overall, these optimisations allow Amazon to offer one day deliveries.

There isn't any definitive published information on the number of users across the various Amazon services[23]. However, it is estimated that over 90% of UK and US shoppers use it with monthly active users up to 600 million. Furthermore, Amazon Prime has 200 million subscribers with 75% of them in the US. Amazon Prime Video had 175 million viewers in 2021. The company reported revenues of $458b in the 12 months ending the 30th of September 2021 (a 31.6% increase compared to the previous 12 months)[24].

Uber

For the third quarter ending 30th September 2021, Uber reported all-time high gross bookings of $23.1bn (up 57% year on year) and revenue of $4.8bn (up 72% year on year)[25]. The Monthly Active Platform Consumers were 109 million (up 40% year on year).

AI has long been at the core of how the company thinks and operates. In 2018, Uber director of product, Jairam Ranganathan said at a conference, 'We don't even think about it anymore, it's kinda like not thinking about computers'[26]. The company uses AI in several areas to optimise operations and offer customers a better service.

Uber uses AI to make more accurate estimated time of arrival (ETA) predictions and to make the most efficient route recommendations to drivers, considering factors such as traffic and weather. Demand forecasting is used to inform drivers, increase supply, to increase prices appropriately and reduce ETA. It leverages these core capabilities to estimate delivery times and maximise delivery efficiencies within Uber Eats. In this context, Uber also uses AI to rank restaurants by user preference. From a 'communication' perspective, AI is used to help with responses customer enquiries resulting in increased efficiency (10%) and customer satisfaction[26]. It also innovated with 'One-Click Chat' that helps drivers reply quickly and safely to customer questions on UberChat by using one click through analysing the query and intent to predict top potential responses.

The company has enabled enterprise level AI development and adoption through focus on two areas[27]. Uber uses a machine learning platform infrastructure called Michelangelo to gather data, manage data pipelines, build, evaluate and deploy models in a standardised and scalable manner. An organisational structure, including groups with key skills required and a community of AI practitioners, assists with supporting processes to ensure accountability and appropriate risk management.

* * *

It is apparent that there are many more AI success stories outside of healthcare than in it. However, there are healthcare examples to be found, and many other early signs of potential. The non-healthcare success stories above provides us with useful context, and insights into what is required for AI to have impact at scale.

CHAPTER 4

HEALTHCARE IS CHANGING

The Covid-19 pandemic emphasised the value of technology, and it shaped both citizen and healthcare professional expectations of how healthcare should and can be delivered.

The impact on healthcare was against a wide backdrop – how we learn, earn a living, buy goods and services we need, and how we enjoy ourselves. Wherever you lived, Covid-19 had an impact on you, your family and friends. Many industries had to evolve, and do so rapidly, to survive, operate in a constrained environment and to meet the changing needs of their users. To do so, technology was critical.

A CATALYST

The London School of Economics and Political Science, in partnership with Confederation of British Industry (CBI), conducted a survey of 425 UK businesses in July 2021, exploring the topic of technology adoption since the start of the pandemic[1]. It showed that 75% of firms had adopted digital technologies since March 2020, with technologies related to sales and marketing (70%), and people management and remote working business functions (66%) being the most frequently adopted.

According to a global chief information officer (CIO) survey conducted by Harvey Nash and KPMG[2] in 2020, an additional spend of 5% of their IT budget was allocated to deal with the pandemic. This equated to an extra $15bn per week during the first three months of the pandemic, resulting in technology spending growing faster than at any point in history.

One industry where change was most profound was retail.

Sundeep Khanna is Chief Strategy Officer at the Landmark Group, one of the largest retail and hospitality organisations in the Middle East, Africa and India. Sundeep is responsible for looking after their retail brands from a corporate perspective, defining projects to take them from strategy to execution. He explains that at one point early during the pandemic, they had to go from a business built on 90% store revenue to a 100% e-commerce retailer.

Thinking and operating as a pure e-commerce player precipitated questions and inventive answers. 'How to shift inventory from retail into online?', 'How to deal with deliveries?', 'How to handle cash payments?' (Cash on delivery is popular in the Middle East).

Landmark's challenge was how to manage the shift in demand for the types of products. For example, with more working from home, customers were buying a lot more comfortable clothes than 'office' clothes.

The Landmark workforce also needed to shift to and adjust to effectively working remotely as a company. Sundeep comes from a consulting background, and is used to working from different locations, but for most of Landmark's workforce, remote working was new.

The healthcare industry also underwent rapid change.

In 2021, Imperial College London's Institute of Global Health Innovation surveyed over 2,200 people working in the health and care sectors across Australia, Italy, India, UAE, UK and the US[3]. The report, commissioned by Ernst and Young, shows that 62% of organisations have increased their use of digital technologies since the onset of the pandemic. Adoption of video conferencing platforms increased from 27% to 73%; the number of organisations offering video consultation increased from 22% to 71%.

Covid-19 accelerated technology adoption in healthcare

Three key drivers facilitated the rapid adoption of technology during Covid-19.

1. **Necessity**

Restrictions introduced by governments to curb the spread of the virus meant citizens (and in some cases healthcare professionals) couldn't travel and attend face to face consultations. Fearful of catching the virus, citizens also didn't want to go to the GP surgery, or to the hospital for an appointment, or to the pharmacy.

A McKinsey analysis in April 2020 reported that 32% of office and outpatient visits in the US were carried out using telehealth[4].

In England, face-to-face GP appointments decreased from 77% in January 2020 to a low of 36% in April 2020. Telephone consultations increased from 18% in January to a maximum of 61% in June. There was no significant change in video consultations, with the percentage actually decreasing after March 2020.

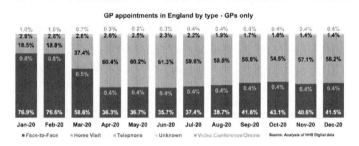

Figure 5: GP appointments in England by type
(GPs only)

The Royal National Orthopaedic Hospital in England provided 11,200 face-to-face outpatient appointments a month across two hospital sites prior to the pandemic[5]. During the pandemic, the hospital planned to reduce face-to-face appointments to only 20% of all appointments and deliver the rest via virtual consultations. It managed to deliver 87% of consultations virtually during the first 6 weeks, however 92% of virtual consultations were telephone consultations rather than video consultations. Patient feedback indicated satisfaction rates of 90/100 for telephone and 85/100 for video consultations, with a clinician satisfaction rate of 78/100 for video consultations.

The Electronic Prescribing Service (EPS) in England enables GPs to send prescriptions directly to a patient-nominated pharmacy that is convenient for the patient, without the need for an FP10 (paper prescription) to be generated, facilitating remote consultations. Primary Care prescribing data from the NHS Business Services Authority (BSA) revealed that use of the EPS service grew rapidly in the initial three years after its introduction, then between 2018 and 2020 the rate of uptake appeared to be on its way to a plateau, with EPS prescriptions making up 77.5% of total prescriptions before the pandemic. The significant leap in electronic prescribing rates, up to 94.15% in 2020/21[6] was a natural consequence of the need to maximise remote consulting in early 2020.

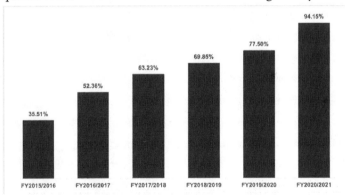

Figure 6: Percentage of items dispensed via EPS in England

An analysis by the Pharmaceutical Journal showed that distance selling pharmacies in England dispensed 42 million items in 2020, which is a 44.8% year-on-year increase[7]. Interestingly, 65% more patients chose a distance selling pharmacy in 2020 relative to 2019 as part of the EPS process above, compared to only a 22% increase for traditional brick and mortar pharmacies during the same period. However, the overall percentage of the market, in terms of total items dispensed in the community, that distance selling pharmacies enjoyed was still low at 4.1%.

YouGov conducted a survey of over 4,000 UK adults and over 1,000 NHS staff in October 2020[8]. The survey revealed a largely positive experience of citizens and NHS staff using technology such as the video consultations or booking appointments online for health care purposes during the COVID-19 pandemic. 83% of citizens had a positive experience, and 78% of NHS staff had a positive experience, which increased to 88% if they had been personally involved in the increase of technology use in the organisation.

Overall positive experiences combined with the increased availability of online health services have helped shape longer term expectations of both citizens and healthcare professionals.

2. **A pragmatic approach to information governance and data governance**

During the pandemic, the need to react quickly to the changing priorities of health services, share data and try new things presented some challenges from a regulation and governance perspective. There was a lack of clarity on what could or could not be done and people were rightly worried.

In the US, there was confusion about the applicability of the Health Insurance Portability and Accountability Act of 1996 (HIPAA) requirements. Federal authorities and the Centers for Disease Control and Prevention (CDC) provided clarification and issued formal guidance on how patient health information may be used, disclosed and shared[9]. At a global level, both the WHO and the UN issued guidance and policy briefs on ethical considerations and human rights related to sharing of information for Covid-19, for example contact tracing.

On a more practical level, the US Centers for Medicare & Medicaid Services (CMS) relaxed rules allowing smartphones to be used for telehealth[10]. This in turn supported the rapid adoption and increase in telehealth activity we highlighted earlier on.

In England, guidance was issued by NHSX (an organisation created in 2019 to drive policy on the use of technology and data within the NHS and now part of the Transformation Directorate within NHS England & Improvement). This guidance (endorsed by the Information Commissioner's Office, National Data Guardian and NHS Digital) provided information for service users, healthcare professionals and IG professionals[11]. It covered a range of use cases including mobile messaging, video conferencing, home working and the use of clinicians' own devices. The guidance also explained the applicability of regulations such as General Data Protection Regulation (GDPR) and Control of Patient Information (COPI).

The Information Commissioner's Office (ICO) issued a statement on 12 March 2020 which laid out a pragmatic approach to interpretation and enforcement of data protection regulation in the context of compelling public interest raised by the pandemic[12]. The ICO and other European Data Protection authorities also issued more detailed guidance.

3. **Resource allocation**

Significant funding was made available during the pandemic to support healthcare systems develop, adopt and scale health technology. This was complemented by changes to support the 'buying' and 'paying' for these. In addition, several suppliers took the opportunity to offer their solutions 'for free', mostly with a view to establish themselves in the market and identify opportunities to commercialise in the longer term.

There have been several examples of funding allocation for specific initiatives. In March 2020, the then NHSX announced a scheme called 'Techforce19' and allocated £0.5m to support technologies that could be scaled up rapidly to support delivery of care during Covid-19[13]. The Scottish government made available £5m to help community pharmacies set up delivery services[14].

Private investors have also been active. According to Rock Health, the total funding for digital health in 2020 was $14.6bn, almost double the $7.9bn raised in 2019[15]. Quarter 1 to Quarter 3 of 2021 saw funding reach $21.3bn, indicating another massive increase during 2021.

NHSX established 'frameworks' to make it easier for NHS organisations in England to buy approved and funded solutions, including secure clinical communication platforms and remote monitoring solutions[16].

In March 2020, the NHS in England and Scotland bought Microsoft Teams for all staff to support collaboration and remote working[17]. NHS England also centrally procured a telehealth solution called Attend Anywhere for 12 months, at a cost of £4.85m, for use by hospitals (RNOH in the above example used this solution)[18]. Changes were made in the US to include telehealth services in reimbursements enabling organisations to get paid for virtual consultations.

There have been more recent funding allocations in 2020/21 budgets to provide continued support for technology adoption. For example, in England an extra £5.9bn was announced in October 2021 of which £2.1bn was to improve IT and digital technology within the NHS[19]. In Wales an extra £25m was allocated to support a £175m investment in strategic digital transformation[20]. In the US, President Joe Biden announced in June 2021 the intention to allocate $80m funding to support Covid-19 related objectives including improving public health technology and COVID-19 data collection[21].

DRIVERS BEFORE COVID-19

Before 2020, healthcare's future was defined by three key drivers. These drivers are still present and we must not forget them as we consider how best to deliver healthcare in a post-Covid world.

An ageing population

According to the Organisation for Economic Co-operation and Development (OECD), the over-65 population is increasing dramatically across the world.

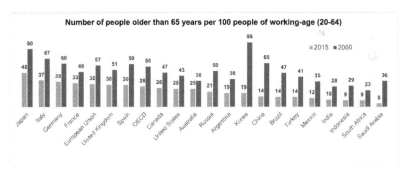

Figure 7: Number of people aged 65 years or older per 100 people of working age (20-64 years)[22]

In 2015, Japan (48), Italy (37) and Germany (35) had the highest number of over 65s compared to 100 people of working age. Indonesia (9), South Africa (9) and Saudi Arabia (5) had the lowest.

The OECD expects that Saudi Arabia's over-65 population in 2060 will be more than six times what it was in 2015. In Korea and China, the over-65 population will more than triple. This results in the predictions that Korea (89), Japan (80) and Italy (67) will have the highest ratio of over 65s in 2060, and Indonesia (29), India (28) and South Africa (23) will have the lowest. Compared to the lowest ratio of older adults to working age adults of 5 per 100 (Saudi Arabia) in 2015, the lowest ratio in 2060 is set to more than triple to 23 per 100, highlighting the overall trend of the increase in the over 65 years population compared to the working age population.

An increase in people with chronic disease, other age-related diseases, and multi-morbidity

The change in age profiles will lead to an increase in the demand for healthcare and strain healthcare delivery.

Older people have more age specific conditions such as dementia and chronic conditions such as heart disease.

When considering people over 65 in the UK, the number estimated to have dementia is expected to increase 80%, from 883,100 in 2019 up to 1,590,100 in 2040[23]. More worryingly, the number with severe dementia increases 109%, from 510,600 in 2019 to 1,066,000 in 2040.

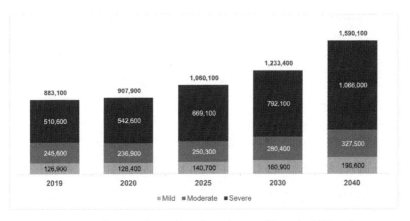

Figure 8: Projected number of people over 65 in the UK with dementia

The British Geriatrics Society defines frailty as the 'distinctive health state related to the ageing process in which multiple body systems gradually lose their in-built reserves'[24]. It worsens an individual's ability to successfully cope with illness. It has also been shown that it increases the risk of falls, disability, care home admission, hospitalisation and death[25]. The risk was higher with severe frailty compared to intermediate frailty.

A survey of Canadian over-65s showed that the prevalence of frailty was 18.6% in men and 25.3% in women. The numbers increased significantly in people over 85 years of age, with 39.1% of men and 45.1% of women being identified as frail.

A systematic review in 2017 revealed an interesting insight – it found that frailty and prefrailty was higher in community-dwelling older adults in upper middle-income countries compared with high-income countries[26]. Pooled frailty and prefrailty prevalence rates, from a majority of upper middle-income economies, were 17.4% and 49.3% compared to 10.7% and 41.6% weighted prevalence previously reported in high-income countries. It also confirmed that frailty was significantly higher in women compared with men.

Multimorbidity is increasing. In 2015, 9.8% of the UK population had four or more chronic conditions, with the number expected to increase to 17% by 2035[27].

Although present in a proportion of younger people, multimorbidities are significantly more present in those over 65 years. A US study reported the prevalence of multimorbidity in people over 65 years to be 67%[28]. It further found that each additional chronic condition was associated especially in those above 75 years, with an increase in the number of functional limitations. It has also been shown that multimorbidity occurs 10 to 15 years earlier in socioeconomically deprived areas[29].

Multimorbidity is particularly complex to manage and requires a wholesale change, because traditional healthcare is organised and delivered with a focus on a single disease. This will also have wider implications on how healthcare professionals are trained and supported, and to how clinical treatment protocols are developed to account for 'combinations' or 'clusters' of diseases to take into account effectiveness and safety of multiple treatment options.

Increasing costs

The reasons behind increasing costs are not as straightforward as they may first appear.

On a most basic level, it appears that health spending per individual increases with age. For example, the analysis by the UK Office for Budget Responsibility (OBR) revealed a five-fold increase in spending between those up to the age of 65 years and patients over 90 years old[30]. Costs considered include provision of primary and secondary care, medication and government capital spending (i.e. building of hospitals).

However, the increase in spending is not solely driven by age. Studies have shown that the increased spending as an individual ages is more closely related to how close that individual is to death, which acts as an indicator for the level of morbidity and therefore the level of care needed[31]. Furthermore, it has been demonstrated that the changing age-mix only increases the per person health spending by 0.6 additional percentage points per year between 2015 and 2050[32]. The authors explain that price growth and technological advancements will be the main accelerators in healthcare expenditure.

Nevertheless, there are specific disease and health elements that are contributing to increasing costs.

Multimorbidity has been shown to increase the use of healthcare services and result in increased costs. A systematic review of UK studies published in 2021 revealed that the most significant impact of multimorbidity is on unplanned hospitalisations, with up to 14.4 times increased odds of an unplanned admission for those with four or more conditions[33]. Although it is more complex to model and based only on two studies, it was also shown that people with up to three conditions account for up to 2.8 times the cost compared to those without any morbidities.

These findings have been confirmed by studies done in China[34], Switzerland[35] and Canada[36]. In the Swiss study, conducted across 229,493 people aged 65 or more, it was found that multimorbidity increased the number of consultations per year (15.7 versus 4.4 in those without morbidity), increased likelihood of hospitalisation by 5.6 times and the total costs by 5.5 times. An additional chronic condition increased costs by 33%.

Second to consider are the demonstrable costs associated with dementia, which are projected to increase significantly over the next 20 years. In the UK, for people over 65 years of age, the total spending for dementia is projected to increase by 171%, from £34.7b in 2019 up to £94.1b in 2040[23].

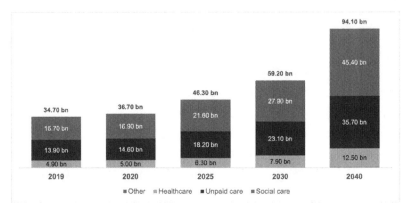

Figure 9: Projected costs for over 65s in the UK with dementia

Costs associated with frailty should also be considered. A study was done in Australia with older people discharged from hospital to a community-based Transition Care Program[37]. It reported that people with an intermediate or high level of frailty (50% and 30% of the cohort) increased the costs of 6 months of health care by 22% and 43% compared with those with low frailty.

A focus on prevention and on utilising technology

Many health systems have been looking at prevention and the use of technology as a means to improve the effectiveness and efficiency of healthcare delivery.

Explicitly prevention-oriented policy-making is evident as far back as 2010. In the US, the Affordable Care Act was passed by Congress and signed by President Obama on the 23rd of March in 2010[38]. The act made preventative interventions more affordable by removing cost-sharing requirements. The changes were also expected to increase access to preventative services for 88 million Americans, with plans expected to offer recommended preventative services including evidence-based screening programmes and vaccinations.

The NHS in England published its Long Term Plan in January 2019[39]. One of the key areas of focus was disease prevention, with plans to support smoking cessation services, alcohol abuse rehabilitation services, diabetes prevention initiatives and disease specific interventions aimed at reducing complication rates, such as expanding the provision of pulmonary rehabilitation with the intention to prevent 500,000 COPD exacerbations over ten years.

A 2019 report by the Institute for Public Policy Research highlights that over 50% of the disease burden in England is preventable, with 20% of deaths attributed to causes that could have been avoided[40]. The report articulates the importance of disease prevention in the future of healthcare provision and contains a number of relevant observations and conclusions. One conclusion was that people value health highly; for example, a King's Fund commissioned survey in 2017 showed that people would be willing to pay more taxes to support NHS spending. The report observed that improved health will have both a positive impact on the workforce, helping create wealth and that it will reduce demand for and therefore the pressure on the NHS and related services.

Prevention is on the agenda of many other nations. Australia published the Long Term National Health Plan in August 2019, which included a 10-year National Preventive Health Strategy[41].

Investment in health innovation

The WHO Global strategy on digital health 2020-2025 (initial draft developed in early 2019 and the final version published in 2021, following consultations and refinement) highlights that there is a 'growing consensus in the global health community that the strategic and innovative use of digital and cutting-edge information and communications technologies will be an essential enabling factor towards ensuring that one billion more people benefit from universal health coverage, that one billion more people are better protected from health emergencies, and that one billion more people enjoy better health and well-being'[42]. The document formalises guiding principles for the promotion of the appropriate use of digital technologies for health and considers health promotion and disease prevention, patient safety, data privacy, patient-centred care, and the adoption of evidence-based interventions and solutions.

In September 2019, the US FDA issued a collection of guidance to support digital health innovation and updated its regulation processes to reflect a more modern approach[43]. One notable change was to take a more risk based approach (based on the negative impact on patients if it malfunctions) to the regulation of clinical decision support (CDS) solutions.

In England in 2019, the government announced £250m funding for the NHS AI Lab to promote collaborative working between the NHS, academics and industry, to develop the use of AI for the improvement of healthcare provision, in line with the NHS Long Term Plan[44]. A related initiative, the Artificial Intelligence (AI) Award, allocated grant funding over 4 years to accelerate the testing and evaluation of promising AI technologies[45].

REDESIGN BY PANDEMIC

As healthcare providers emerge from the pandemic, we must take time to reflect on our experiences, and the advances that helped us through the turbulent times. Many initiatives and technologies were implemented quickly, to meet specific requirements created by the pandemic (i.e. the ability to conduct consultations remotely because of social distancing). This has provided a great foundation, proving what can be done. However, what worked in that particular environment may not be suitable in the longer term and the risk-benefit analysis that was applicable during the unprecedented Covid-19 times may no longer be valid. With the demonstration of inequality of Covid-19 outcomes by race (i.e. African-American patients in the US having a higher mortality rate[46]), we must also carefully consider how and who innovation is benefiting, to ensure health inequalities are not worsened.

When considering the longer term, we should not forget the difficulties facing healthcare before the pandemic. We should consider how the pandemic (and how we managed through it) has changed the landscape in which healthcare will be delivered in the future – the 'redesign' as a result of the pandemic. The pandemic shone a light on certain cracks in global healthcare systems. In the US, it highlighted the inadequacies of a funding system based on employment-linked health insurance policies during furlough and redundancies[47]. Providers who were already facing significant financial pressure were hit further, through additional costs, and the necessary deferment of the majority of elective care. When looking to the future, as well as to the 'system' – care delivery, supporting processes, funding, and technology – we must absolutely not forget the workforce who worked tirelessly during the pandemic.

As we come out of the eye of the storm, focus will shift to a number of key themes:

1. **Post Covid recovery**

   During Covid-19 the focus was, rightly, on urgent care delivery. This resulted in routine care and elective procedures, such as orthopaedics procedures, including knee and hip replacements, being put on hold. Backlogs and waiting lists have grown significantly.

   The total waiting list for specialist treatment in England was 5.98 million at the end of October 2021[48]. This was a 41%

increase from the number of people on the waiting list at the start of the pandemic and the first lockdown in the country in March 2020. Worryingly, this increase was despite a sharp drop in the number of patients being added to the waiting list during March 2020 (30% drop compared to March 2019). Waiting list additions only started to recover to pre-Covid levels in March 2021. 21.3 million referrals were added to the waiting list between March 2020 and July 2021, but if we consider the same months before the pandemic started, in which there were 28.7 million waiting list additions, assuming referrals would have otherwise continued at the same rate, there are potentially more than 7.4 million extra patients 'missing' from the waiting list.

Of the 5.98 million that were on the waiting lists at the time, patients waiting for trauma and orthopaedics treatment are the most common, making up 12% of the list. A study was conducted with questionnaires being sent to 888 patients on the English patients on the elective orthopaedic waiting list[49]. Of the respondents, 82% had tried self-help and 94% still wanted to have the planned procedure, with only 21% willing to defer treatment. Understandably, 'frustrated', 'pain', 'disappointed', and 'not happy/depressed' were frequent responses related to questions about mood.

The study's authors suggest a pragmatic solution to address the findings, consisting of a 3-tiered approach. They proposed to better understand the *concerns* of patients through providing direct phone lines to the waiting list team, the use of video conferencing technology to provide better access to clinicians and to make access to triage more accessible through flexible clinic slots. The second part of the solution focused on the provision of support to help patients *cope,* through signposting them to relevant information or by providing community pain management and physiotherapy services. The last recommendation was to enable better *catch-up* for patients on the waiting list via text message updates and by developing a live dashboard on the hospital website.

An approach such as the above will also allow two other important points to be addressed, as highlighted by Patel et al[50]. The first is to keep attention on clinical prioritisation, which may need to be changed if the patient's condition changes (independently of how long they have been on the waiting list for). The second is to take the opportunity of every interaction with the patient to promote health prevention and wellbeing and to identify and manage risks associated with comorbidities and chronic conditions.

Neville Young points to cancer and cardiovascular disease as two of the biggest causes of death and that falling behind on early diagnosis on these, as happened during the last pandemic, is presenting a real challenge now. He says that these two areas will be a huge focus for ICS and therefore 'ripe for innovation'. This may include using the data we have in a different way and using AI (but not necessarily always AI) to better understand the waiting lists and to prioritise patients according to their clinical need.

Tackling the huge waiting lists will require extra funding. The NHS in England allocated £2bn in 2021 to help with Covid-19 backlogs and waiting lists[51]. It additionally funded a £160 million initiative to trial new ways of working, including a high-volume cataract service, one stop testing facilities, better access for GPs to obtain specialist advice and 'Super Saturday' clinics. Lancashire and South Cumbria ICS will be using the funding to further develop an AI based solution to prioritise the appropriate level of care and support for patients on waiting lists.

2. **Funding and efficiency**

The Health Foundation estimates that the NHS in England will require approximately £10b extra funding by 2023/24[52]. This will include the planned investment of £3bn a year in public health, £1bn in workforce training and £1bn in capital, comprised entirely of extra funding, to meet the rising demand for mental health services and to deliver against the NHS Long Term Plan.

As highlighted by Waitzberg et al, during the Covid 19 pandemic, governments across the US, England, Germany, and Israel provided financial support to the health providers with the majority of support for providers who relied on public payments. The authors also relate that systems based on activity based payments are more vulnerable during a pandemic, when activity volumes and elective procedures will be greatly reduced (compared to those operating on a capitation budget for providing services to a population). The authors also note that activity based payments will incentivise providers to develop new, safe, ways to deliver services that are not impacted by pandemic restrictions – for example, telemedicine based services. A wider point, not discussed in the paper, is the further weight that the pandemic provides for the argument to move to a health funding system based on capitated budgets and outcomes, providing better security for providers and driving better outcomes for patients and payers.

A World Bank report paints a darker picture[53]. It highlighted that 163 million people would be in extreme poverty by the end of 2021, taking global poverty rates back to 2015 levels. After most countries increased health spending in response to the pandemic, it predicts that most government spending will fall in 2021 and in 2022, mainly due to the inability for many governments to borrow further. The report suggests a range of measures that governments could consider including spending reviews/performance based budgets, external financing options, pro-health tax reforms, accessing debt relief and maximising the efficiency of the health spending.

For governments to allocate extra funding in the longer term, especially where public debt has increased significantly to meet the short term demands of the pandemic, tax increases such as those to be implemented in England from April 2022 may be necessary.

Maximising the efficiency of health spending will be key, and approaching this through new ways of delivering care and promoting prevention and self-management will be more sustainable than just cost-cutting.

Karen Johnson is the Finance Director at Gloucestershire Hospitals NHS Foundation Trust in England. She says, 'money wasn't the barrier' during the pandemic, compared to the years before the pandemic when there was a strong focus on making efficiency savings. She explains that she maintained appropriate governance throughout, because even though the money was available, they still had an obligation to spend it in the most cost-effective way possible. For her, it has always been about making the right decisions for the patients: 'What are the outcomes?', 'How do we measure them?', 'How do we know when the outcomes have been achieved?' During the pandemic, this principle became even more important as the hospital was procuring things very quickly.

While she feels it would be 'a shame' to go back to the pre-pandemic environment of cost efficiency drives, Karen says that spending has gone up significantly during the pandemic and that everyone knows that the NHS now needs to get their finances under control. Karen explains that the priority is now is to drive productivity by working smarter, in a more automated and effective way.

3. **New ways of delivering care**

Dr Shantanu Nundy explains his vision for a 'distributed, digitally enabled, and decentralised' health system in the US[54]. Distributed care is the practice of delivering care closer to the patient, in their homes and out in their communities, rather than being constrained to hospitals and health clinics. Digitally enabled care makes different care models possible with 24/7 access to relevant resources and support, better sharing of metrics such as glucose levels between patients and clinicians, and connecting with other similar patients to share experiences and learnings. Decentralised care seeks to empower patients and healthcare professionals to make decisions and spend to provide what the patient would most benefit, from rather than be dependent on what the insurance company would reimburse.

With the increasing focus on regional care and the legislation and formalisation of expectations of ICSs in England, another reconfiguration is on the cards – of organisations, people, service delivery and supporting functions. There is hope that joined-up care will be developed that benefits from the learnings, best practice and positive outcomes from Covid-19, and that it will be an opportunity to consider a citizen journey across care settings. In addition, a move from an activity based payment model to a capitated budget based on population health outcomes is a possibility with further advantages as highlighted above. This type of care delivery model could also facilitate a 'distributed, digitally enabled, and decentralised' health system as Dr Shantanu Nundy envisages.

In redesigning new care models, underlying drivers that were defining the future of healthcare before the pandemic (and that remain unchanged), and those that we have already covered, must not be forgotten.

Let's revisit YouGov's October 2020 survey[55]. 42% of service users and 33% of staff said that technology made the traditional ways of delivering care and communicating worse. This merits a pause and reflection, to understand more about the reasons for these opinions before embedding the technologies 'as-is' into long term care delivery models. This is especially true if we consider that the majority of virtual consultations by both English GPs and in the RNOH examples were in fact telephone consultations rather than video consultations. One of the key considerations is whether to seek to adopt virtual versus face-to-face versus hybrid delivery models. It is likely that hybrid models are most likely to be the most effective and appropriate. This is a trend beginning to emerge in mergers and acquisitions activity reported by Rock Health[56]. It reported in November 2021 that virtual care company Thirty Madison opened its first brick-and-mortar location and that Dallas's Parkland Health and Hospital System selected digital platform Current Health to develop its hypertension monitoring program.

The digitisation of healthcare should not widen existing health inequalities. A review of studies published during the first wave of Covid-19 revealed that the elderly and ethnic minorities faced known difficulties in using digital healthcare services[57]. Appropriate user research must inform the development of digital health solutions and supporting (non-digital) services must be considered to maximise the number of people that a digital service can benefit.

On a related note, we must be cautious that some of the decisions regarding risk and governance, appropriately made during the pandemic, do not have unintended adverse effects long term. For example, the relaxation of IG requirements resulted in reduced demand for the secure communication platform for healthcare professionals being offered by a fledgling start-up. Sadly, the developers closed down its service in January 2022[58].

4. **Prevention and self management**

The pandemic has reinforced awareness of the value of prevention, and of public health. This will be an increased priority for many health systems.

Research conducted by GSK and Ipsosin mid-2020, with 4,400 participants aged between 16 and 75 in Germany, Italy, Spain and the UK, revealed interesting results[59]. It showed that 65% of people are now more likely to consider their health in day-to-day decision-making. It also demonstrated that a large proportion of people consider it important to take their health into their own hands to relieve pressure on healthcare systems – 84% in Spain, 77% in the UK, 75% in Italy and 63% in Germany.

University College London (UCL) partners in England have developed a set of care frameworks to help GPs proactively manage long term conditions such as heart disease, strokes, asthma and COPD[60]. It includes tools to risk-stratify and pathways to effectively manage high risk patients, including maximising remote delivery of care, training to support the workforce deliver personalised care and, importantly, it identifies elements of care that can be delivered by healthcare professionals other than the already stretched GPs.

Prevention-oriented thinking raises an intriguing question: can patients be incentivised, through reimbursement models and insurance premium discounts (as well as different methodologies in non-insurance payer models), to self-manage their chronic conditions?[61]. If a patient with Type 2 Diabetes was provided with feedback on their glucose levels and energy expenditure, would it help them to modify their diet and exercise regimen?

5. **A depleted workforce**

The King's Fund reports that there are an estimated 100,000 vacancies across the NHS in England that cannot be filled[62]. The pandemic continues to cause further short staff shortages during the traditionally busiest times for the NHS (due to the cold weather and associated increase in illnesses). On 19 December 2021, it was reported that 18,829 NHS staff at hospitals were absent due to reasons related to Covid-19, more than 51% of the number absent at the beginning of December[63]. This creates a very stressful environment.

A US study from the spring and summer of 2020 reveals that there was an increase in attrition and retirement of nurses due to challenging working conditions[64].

Many, including the British Medical Association, have made the point that extra funding by itself will not help to fix issues (i.e. an extra £160 million to help reduce waiting lists) if parallel steps are not put in place to help support an exhausted workforce[65].

The King's Fund further reports that the NHS People Plan published in August 2020 did not provide the comprehensive strategy needed in order to help overcome the workforce challenges. It recommends that recruitment and retention be improved with attractive pay, opportunities for flexible working and clearer career pathways. It also highlights that the workforce needs time to recover, with paid leave and access to psychological support where needed, and for their workplaces to be supportive environments with cultures and leaders who model and are committed to compassion, inclusion and collaboration.

The workforce also needs support and training to deliver care effectively in the healthcare landscape redesigned by the pandemic and to safely maximise the use of technology and digitally enabled healthcare.

CHAPTER 5

IT'S NOT EASY BEING A MACHINE: TRUST AND ACCOUNTABILITY WITH NEW TECHNOLOGY

Let's revisit the controversy surrounding Khosla's prediction that AI would replace 80% of doctors.

Khosla generated anger, and comments like 'Health care is like witchcraft and just based on tradition'[1]. There was acknowledgement of his wider points, for example by US physician Davis Liu, that healthcare delivery can be more consistent and systematic, resulting in reliable outcomes for every patient.

David Parkes, George F. Colony Professor of Computer Science and co-director of the Harvard Data Science Initiative notes that AI as a technology has been in medicine since the 1970s[2]. For example, expert systems such as MYCIN to help doctors better diagnose and manage bacterial infection. However, David explains that while MYCIN was as good as 'human experts' at the specific task, the system was 'brittle, hard to maintain, and too costly'.

The other point that Khosla raised was that the disruption of healthcare would be driven from outside, much like Jack Dorsey disrupted payments with Square[3]. Khosla's central prediction hasn't translated into reality, with AI adoption within healthcare still in early stages, with only pockets of innovation and use.

The lack of adoption is reflected in academic publication where the majority of studies into AI use in healthcare are retrospective and many are of early and small scale evaluations. For example, a review of such studies published between 2000 and 2018 revealed that 98% of the 386 studies were retrospective and mostly limited to proof of concept approaches[4].

A European Union report published in 2021 reviewed the development, adoption and use of AI in healthcare across its member states[5]. The study found while most had developed AI strategies identifying health as a priority, they were not translated to specific policies. Further, while they were open to adoption, actual adoption was limited to specific departments and use cases. Barriers to adoption included lack of trust, difficulty with integration into current workflows, and lack of funding for development or licensing solutions.

Would you recommend robot-assisted surgery to a loved one?

A review of studies published between 2000 and 2020 explored AI acceptability as one of the key themes[6]. AI acceptability was assessed using various elements including trust, satisfaction, willingness to use again and willingness to recommend to family and friends. While the overall sentiment towards AI was positive, accuracy and privacy were areas where participants had reservations. Many participants viewed the currently available AI as 'premature technology'.

A YouGov poll of more than 2,000 adults in March 2021 revealed more insights into the types of 'services' people may be willing to accept from AI or robots[7]. The most acceptable services were robots filling prescriptions (40%), robot-assisted surgery (37%) and diagnosis of illnesses through analysing investigations (26%). 23% were willing to receive GP services (such as the treatment of common conditions or general medical advice) and urgent or intensive care. Notably, 34% said they would not be willing to receive any of the services stated.

An additional nuance to the above figures is digital exclusion, resulting in experiences that can vary across different groups. Digital exclusion can occur if people don't have the skills to use digital devices, or do not have access to the internet or appropriate devices, or if the digital service isn't designed considering their needs (including those who need support through non-digital means)[8]. According to Ofcom, while some elements of the 'digital divide' appear to have narrowed during Covid-19 (for example, the proportion of homes without internet access has reduced from 11% in March 2020 to 6%

in March 2021), significant disparities still exist[9]. The broadcasting and telecoms regulator pointed out that for the 6% households that remained offline, the negative impact during the lockdown would have been greater. Additionally, those that have the least access are some of the most disadvantaged or at risk (for example, 18% of those over 65, 11% of lower income households and 10% of the most financially vulnerable). To encourage equitable uptake, we also need to be aware of differing attitudes and perceived benefits. For example, a survey conducted by the Ada Lovelace Institute of 2,023 UK adults in early 2021 asking about attitudes towards technologies deployed during the COVID-19, found that people with disabilities or identifying themselves as clinical vulnerable felt personal fitness and mental wellbeing apps were less likely to be effective.

Machine learning advances are also uncovering new concerns about trust and privacy. A 2018 study demonstrated that with ML techniques, it was possible to identify individuals from anonymised US data, prompting questions whether 1996's HIPAA (Health Insurance Portability and Accountability Act) legislation needs to be updated[10]. The researchers used techniques such as support vector machine (SVM) and random forests to re-identify 80% of children's and 95% of adult's physical activity data from a de-identified dataset (where activity data was aggregated into 20-minute intervals) from 14,451 individuals. Another example was from 2012 when Target stores in the US used AI to predict which customers were pregnant based on shopping data, and then sent out coupons for nappies and other parenting and baby products[11]. Although there were clear ethical issues related to consent and customer awareness on how their data was being used, this was not a breach under HIPAA rules as Target was not a 'covered entity'.

A history of ethical failures in Big Tech

Big Tech companies have been at the centre of several controversies. In 2015, Google Photos' automated tagging function mistakenly identified Brooklyn resident Jacky Alciné and his friend, both of whom are black, as 'gorillas'[12]. In 2016, within 24 hours of being released, Microsoft's Twitter bot 'Tay' tweeted a barrage of misogynistic and racist comments[13]. In 2016, US regulators investigated Tesla when an accident killed the driver of a Tesla Model S driven under auto-pilot mode[14].

I was surprised and disappointed by Amazon, a company trusted by millions of people (including myself) with a wide variety of personal data on preferences and lifestyle choices[15]. Seemingly accelerated by an unrelenting drive towards customer-focused innovation and many small teams, there were accounts of lax data security measures, uncontrolled data sharing and unfettered access internally, resulting in the inappropriate access of data, such as employees looking at celebrity purchase histories, and misuse of data (the sabotage of certain seller accounts, for example).

In healthcare, DeepMind (acquired by Google in 2014) made the news regarding patient consent during developing the 'Streams' application (an app to identify and manage acute kidney disease in patients) at the Royal Free NHS Trust in London. The Information Commissioner's Office (ICO) in the UK found that the NHS trust didn't obtain the necessary consent from 1.6m patients when transferring their data to DeepMind to test the app in 2015 and 2016[16]. Although the ICO ruling didn't directly find fault with DeepMind (as the NHS Trust was the 'data controller' and therefore responsible for the data and related regulation), the company released a blog post indicating that they had got some things wrong[17]. The law firm Mishcon de Reya launched a class action lawsuit against DeepMind in October 2021 on behalf of the lead plaintiff, Andrew Prismal, and the remaining 1.6m patients[18].

More generally, there is nervousness regarding the increasing power and influence of Big Tech when it comes to healthcare data and how this may be misused.

Maxine Mackintosh is currently the Programme Lead for Diverse Data at Genomics England. Her previous experience includes being a post-doctoral researcher at the Alan Turing Institute, a Technology & Data Science Expert Consultant for the WHO and on the Independent Review Board for the DeepMind involvement at the Royal Free. She points out that if a company owns the railroads, owns the data infrastructure, and has the knowledge and the assets to build increasingly more complex models, that they have an unfair advantage. For example, the surveillance that Google is capable of doing for public health is far greater than Public Health England (now replaced by the UK Health Security Agency and the Office for Health Improvement and Disparities). She cautions that we need to be very conscious about where the concentrations of power, skills and data are happening, because a public system cannot keep up with major multinational technology companies and that we need to work out a viable and sustainable model for the NHS to work with big and small businesses.

Maneesh Juneja draws attention to a topic not widely discussed, the environmental impact of AI, when 'the NHS is the first health care system in the world to commit to net zero'. He highlights the significant carbon footprint and energy needed to acquire data, train models and store data. Training AI models can have a carbon footprint equivalent to five times the emissions of a car over its lifetime[19].

Maneesh also points out further impact with remote patient monitoring, and wearable and sensor devices (including the carbon footprint associated with manufacturing and recycling these devices). He suggests that we need to start thinking about environmental impact during procurements and when selecting suppliers. Is the race to deploy AI in healthcare going to derail efforts to reach net zero?

It's not all about the technology

The design, development and implementation of AI solutions successfully in healthcare involves many factors beyond the technical ones. Failure to acknowledge this is a grave mistake. When considering the potential of AI in healthcare and analysing early successes, focus was largely on the technical elements – for example, the accuracy of a model. In these instances, it was the translation of that potential or early success from 'in silico' (performed on a computer) to the patient bedside or clinical frontline that failed. And failed miserably, at that.

Socio-technical systems design (STSD) methods have been described as a design approach 'that considers human, social and organisational factors, as well as technical factors'[20]. In this definition, 'organisational' was referring to the organisation itself and "social" was referring to the relationships between people who work together within and across organisations.

While a complex approach can be taken in applying STSD to AI, I choose a more direct application. The most notable benefit is the ability to consider the impact and needs beyond technology, to include individuals (patients, healthcare professionals and operational staff) and processes or context (clinical workflows and funding flows as well as organisational factors including culture). Therefore, when considering the key challenges, I will use three categories – human, operating environment, and technology and data.

AI won't replace doctors anytime soon. There are many challenges related to developing and implementing AI in healthcare. Some relate to technology in general, some relate to healthcare, and only some are related to AI itself.

Only human

Healthcare is deeply personal and important to human beings. Therefore, it is not surprising that, when it comes to matters related to your own health or the health of someone you love, extra scrutiny is applied to the care received and the decisions related to it.

Culture and acceptance

Every industry has its norms and expectations. Healthcare is not different with doctors, nurses, allied healthcare professionals (for example physiotherapists), hospital administrators and non-clinical staff all having strong values and being committed to helping patients get better. Innovators need to appreciate this, be able to navigate the specificities and build trusted relationships. This is not easy, especially if you come from 'outside' healthcare.

Over the last 16 months, Chalinda has reviewed around 400 pitch decks of start-ups seeking investment and thinks about 35% of them mention AI somewhere in the pitch. Chalinda further explains that most of the time he doesn't see any issues with the technology, but that one of the biggest limitations is the founder's understanding of the domain. When it comes to evaluation, he places around 70% emphasis on the team and considers two key elements. The first of these is what he calls the 'founder-market fit', where Chalinda seeks to understand whether the founder will be able to work with the people in the industry. In healthcare, this is whether founders can work with doctors and nurses.

The second key element Chalinda assesses in a start-up proposal is whether the founder is able to really understand the pain points in healthcare, and able to develop and present a useful proposal. Considering how this aspect might be relevant to our own proposals, we need to understand who we are working with and how it might impact them (and therefore, what may be their concerns?). For example, fear of job losses can be a strong deterrent.

Recalling his work with Qure.ai, Rizwan explains that many companies contacted him during the start of the pandemic to offer various AI-driven products. After email discussions and conversations with several of them, he came to the conclusion that many of them did not have a viable use case – for example, claiming to "diagnose" Covid when no one at the time really knew the extent of manifestations of Covid-19 on a CXR[21]. He further explains that many were looking for a use for their product instead of identifying a problem to solve[22]. For example, focusing on cost savings and replacing radiologists, which doesn't go down well when pitching to radiologists!

15 focus groups conducted in late 2019 and early 2020 with 87 patients from the Midwest in the US revealed that, while patients were generally enthusiastic about AI in healthcare, they had several concerns[23]. The concerns included the safety of AI, with an evident desire for human healthcare professionals to retain final discretion, choice (whether they could opt out of having AI involved in their care delivery), data bias, the potential for increasing the cost of already expensive healthcare and data security, and technology failures. The authors of the study warn of potential bias in the sample surveyed, being higher educated than the typical population, however the study provides insights into some of the concerns patients have.

Trust, confidence, and transparency

Healthcare professionals and patients need to have trust and confidence that the AI will be both accurate and arrive at decisions and recommendations in a sensible way.

One of the key enablers to developing trust and confidence, especially for healthcare professionals, is being able to better understand 'how the AI solutions work'. This is referred to as explainability and can be thought of as a spectrum of activities from providing more information related to the decision (accuracy, confidence levels, and so on), visualising the 'defect' or the 'area of interest', to providing more information about what variables were considered, and with which weightings. As we have seen, deep learning techniques have driven a significant proportion of the technical advances in the field of AI. This presents a challenge for explainable solutions, with neural networks-based models being more difficult to understand in terms of 'why' and 'how' a decision was made (i.e. they are 'black boxes').

Engagement and ownership

Related to being able to trust and accept AI solutions, is the feeling of 'being part of' and 'involved'. This boils down to engagement with the design, (co-)development and implementation of AI projects.

Engagement with healthcare professionals, industry operators and management, and patients is often an afterthought, and suboptimal engagement typical. Interested parties not being engaged, or engaged late in the process, leads to difficulties, with time lost trying to solve the wrong 'problem', limiting buy-in, and the development of solutions that actually result in an increased burden on providers and patients, and potentially lead to patient harm.

Skills and knowledge

AI is still new in healthcare, and for many people, it is an unknown beyond what they may have seen in the media. AI does not feature in healthcare undergraduate degrees or as part of the formal training programmes when they start working in clinical practice.

When it comes to initially engaging with design and development, or making decisions among the options available, healthcare professionals or managers who have a modest knowledge of AI may not have an adequate understanding to fully evaluate or to feel comfortable engaging in the process. Second, when it comes to using developed AI software, they feel less confident in 'operating' within the environment, and have less awareness of its limitations and potential pitfalls.

Time and 'headspace'

The delivery of health and care to patients is a 24/7 job. It's a high-stakes environment with extremely high quality standards and expectations of those that deliver services. In this environment, it is hard for healthcare professionals and operational managers to fully engage with innovation on top of their day jobs. For most of them, there is no protected or allocated time for them to get involved with and support these initiatives. It is done during lunch breaks, during evenings or weekends.

Dr Matt Stammers started working with AXIS (Access Extract Integrate Safe data), part of the NIHR Southampton Biomedical Research Centre in 2018. In 2020, he was about to start a PhD; instead, he became the Covid-19 analyst at the Southampton hospital. After successfully leading on modelling work, he was appointed as a substantive consultant in Gastroenterology and data science at University Hospital Southampton. Matt is fully employed by the hospital and splits his time 50:50 on clinical and data science work.

Matt describes the operational pressure on the front line. He says that the demands of the day tend to overtake thinking 'What could be in the future?' He further explains that it is sometimes hard to link the success of the AI to alleviating the pressures of the day job (in some cases, it's easier, – for example, x-ray interpretation), thus most are disincentivised to even acknowledge it.

This constraint adds unwelcome pressure to these individuals and overall reduces the number of professionals that may otherwise be involved and contribute to the successful design, development and implementation of AI tools. As we discuss later, their involvement and support is crucial in the sustainable adoption of AI in healthcare.

Furthermore, feeling as they need to fit these activities around their core work may mean that it's difficult to give the quality of attention and input they could potentially provide.

Human-machine interaction

How AI and healthcare professionals 'work together' to deliver health-care is a really important subject, and one littered with potential stumbling blocks.

One study reviewed how clinicians' antidepressant-prescribing performance was affected by recommendations from a machine learn-ing based solution[24]. It found that the ML system recommendations did not significantly improve clinicians' performance. Worryingly, it found that incorrect recommendations from the system, combined with explanations, and limited but easily interpretable information, led to a significant reduction in performance.

COMPLEXITIES WITH THE OPERATING ENVIRONMENT

Narrow focus

AI is sometimes better than humans at certain medical tasks, such as detecting a bleed from an MRI scan of the brain.

Dr Matt Stammers identifies one of the biggest problems with AI is a 'brittleness', which results from the solution solving one specific thing. This is what we call narrow focus. If the wrong tool is chosen then it is not generally useful, and people can 'break' them too easily. Humans can generalise across problems, whereas AI can't do that right now. There are problems that are happily solved by AI (for example, interpretation of x-rays), but they tend to be either niche or human-in-the loop as a result of this brittleness.

For example, a deep learning algorithm developed by researchers at Google AI achieved 94% accuracy when detecting lung cancer in chest CTs[25]. Comparing model accuracy with that of six experienced radiologists, with eight years of experience on average, and when prior CT scans were not available, the model outperformed all of the radiologists with absolute reductions of 12% in false positives (instances where there no abnormalities in the image but the model/radiologist says there is) and 5% in false negatives (instances where there are abnormalities in the image but the model or radiologist doesn't pick them up). The validation was only done with six radiologists, but the wider point is that if a radiologist was given a CT scan, they would be able to review the images for other abnormalities, not just the lung cancer lesions the model was looking for. This is AI's narrow focus in action. Radiologists don't just focus on one element; they are good at interpreting many different elements of a medical image, and in the context of the wider patient history and other investigations the patient may have had (for example, blood tests).

Let's explore this further. A 2022 study conducted a preclinical evaluation of a DL model to detect hip fractures in x-rays, external validation with data from another hospital and then conducted an audit to identify any variances in the model behaviour[26]. The model performed better than five radiologists (AUC 0·994 compared to 0·969). While it performed strongly in the external validation (AUC 0·980), it would require some adjusting based on each local implementation environment to choose the operating points (a trade-off between the sensitivity and specificity). The audit also identified some concerning findings questioning whether the solution would be safe for clinical implementation. For example, it did not diagnose a significant fracture that a human would have picked up due to the amount of 'displacement' of the bone fragments. Where there were abnormal bones (because of underlying disease, for example), the error rate was significantly higher than with human radiologists. This would not be expected very often, due to the low incidence of the diseases or circumstances, but the study illustrates the importance of considering factors beyond 'accuracy' and in understanding the impact of possible errors.

Dr Michael George is a clinical fellow in data engineering at University Hospital Southampton who works closely with Matt. He explains that clinicians are often not aware of narrow focus, or the care you need when deploying AI in a different setting to ensure there is no harm caused.

Fragmented solutions

Narrow focus translates to innovators and companies focusing on different aspects. Since limited structures exist for companies to collaborate, this often means that each company is trying to solve a problem on its own. This leads to incomplete solutions, meaning that patients and healthcare systems don't get to benefit from holistic technology and that each individual company finds it more difficult to demonstrate a value proposition in the context of a solution that is feasible in real life.

Creating extra demand

AI can inadvertently create extra and unwarranted demand within healthcare systems.

The first way it can do this is through the additional detection of abnormalities. For example, more advanced (and accurate) diagnostic capabilities can lead to an increase in lesions and potentially suspicious areas being flagged up in medical images that would have not been picked up by human readers. A proportion of these would certainly be beneficial to have been identified, or identified earlier, because prompt intervention leads to better clinical outcomes for patients. However, in some cases, it is still not clear whether it leads to better clinical outcomes or whether it merely results in increased anxiety for patients and extra demands on already stretched healthcare systems. More large scale studies are needed to fully investigate these instances.

The second cause of this additional demand is 'alerting' systems. These can flag up risks and potential abnormalities by monitoring and analysing data from wearables (Apple Watch and heart rate monitoring flagging up instances of atrial fibrillation) and other instances where a patient may be identified as requiring clinical attention. In these instances, it is often a tricky balance of identifying where the 'threshold' for the alerts lie, to provide assurance to patients and healthcare professionals when the system does not 'alert', and avoid creating too many alerts of which some are 'false'.

Regulation

Johan Ordish is the Head of Software and AI, Innovative Devices Division, at the MHRA (Medicines and Healthcare products Regulatory Agency) in the UK. Russell Pearson is the NHS AI Liaison Manager in the division. They describe their role as regulating all software as a medical device, including diagnostics and direct-to-consumer products in the UK, with a primary focus on safety. At a high level, they view the scope in two buckets – software as a device and software in a device. AI is considered as a subgroup of software, rather than a separate entity.

Johan and Russell explain that regulation is tricky for innovators. There is a preconception that everything can be turned into a checklist; in reality it is highly interpretable and needs to be contextualised according to the solution and situation. There are things that the innovator can't control – for example, there is wider shared responsibility with clinical decision support systems (who interacts with it and how). Another regulatory challenge is related to making changes to solutions once assured, and striking a balance between assuring the changes versus improving the solution, and realising the benefits.

They also consider the regulator's perspective. First, things are evolving in the field of AI and the state of art is not settled. Second, the evidence base for AI is often weak compared to drugs and medical devices. There are the interpretability and generalisation challenges related to evidencing 'black box' solutions.

Effective and pragmatic regulation is necessary for safe implementation and continual operation of AI solutions. 'Software as a medical device', as applicable to non-AI digital health solutions, is still in its infancy and AI adds further complexity due to its unique relationship with data. Although both the FDA in the US and MHRA in the UK have started to develop guidance, it is far from being mature.

The AI product lifecycle adds complexity to the regulatory framework. For example, AI solutions need to be monitored once deployed and could either change due to the 'learning' nature of the algorithms or driven by the need to update the algorithms to take into account a change in the operating environment – a concept known as drift (for example, change in best practice or a dramatic change in disease landscape or operations driven by exceptional events such as the Covid-19 pandemic).

Accountability

Does the AI solution support humans to make a decision, or does it act autonomously to take action? In either case, regulation is still evolving as to who is responsible and therefore, liabilities if something goes wrong.

This can be further complicated when there is lack of transparency around 'making decisions' and therefore clinicians can't evaluate or further refine insights offered by the AI[11]. In this instance, if an error occurs which results in patient harm, where does the accountability lie? With the organisation that developed the solution, the organisation that implemented and uses it, the healthcare professional, or jointly?

Funding

As is common with digital health technology in general, the questions are 'Who pays for it?' and 'How much?' It is often the case that benefits are seen in another healthcare setting to which it is deployed: for example, a solution deployed in primary care preventing acute admissions to hospital may benefit payers (and in some cases providers in terms of demand management). Equally, when deployed directly with patients, there are likely to be questions on which part of the healthcare ecosystem should pay for it. As described earlier, most healthcare systems operate on an activity based payment system, where some of the benefits digital health and AI can deliver are harder to 'quantify'. It is also often the case that the benefits take some time to be realised, for example invest this financial year and realise benefits in following years. This could be an issue when many healthcare organisation financial planning is done on a yearly basis.

Funding also means procurement and payment mechanisms. There *is* progress when it comes to digital health, with approved tools receiving defined reimbursement amounts and 'frameworks' and other procurement vehicles for healthcare organisations to buy them (and get paid for using them). AI is not quite there yet and issues around clear value proposition, benefits estimation, and regulation to ensure safe operations are being worked through.

Understanding of the domain

Returning to Chalinda Abeykoon's work, he explains that industries, including healthcare, will need to change existing processes for AI to work. He feels that many people are good at building models in very controlled environments, on their computers, but that very few take it out to their target industry and spend the time to really understand how the industry operates. He asks, do the founders really have a desire to understand how the industry works? Do they really want to understand what the problem is? Chalinda explains that when you scratch beneath the surface, the 'problem' can be symptoms of the problem, and the actual problem boils down to processes within the organisations, the people and what's important to them.

Integration into the workflows

Alongside the factors above is the importance of understanding and integrating as far as possible with existing clinical workflows and pathways. This helps reduce unnecessary work for healthcare professionals, gains their buy-in and increases the likelihood of a successful implementation.

Neville Young recalls the implementation of PinPoint. The challenge had nothing to do with technology; it was related to the practicalities of blood sample capture and transport. 'How can they get the blood samples from the GP to the lab?' 'Do they keep the samples together in the fridge and send them at the end of the day or the end of the week?' 'How much will each option cost?' 'Do we need to consider appropriate compensation for GPs who will be doing additional work, if they have now to draw blood from a patient for this test?' Some questions are only realised when new innovations are introduced in real world settings. The expectation that new technologies will always need some adaption to their new environment is a sensible approach for innovators.

TECHNOLOGY AND DATA IN HEALTHCARE IS COMPLICATED

Unlike the industries and use cases highlighted in *Success stories*, the healthcare industry is not blessed with the easily available or accessible, structured, and good (well, decent) quality data.

Healthcare lags behind many other industries in terms of digital technology. Many countries and health systems still use paper records or basic digital systems that make extracting data at scale hard to do. For example, a review in 2018 revealed that 23% hospitals in England were still using paper records[27].

The related challenge is data ownership where data is held within various systems, within proprietary systems and databases, and under various commercial agreements. Lack of integration across different technology systems makes it difficult to share data.

Dr Rushika Fernandopulle is a primary care doctor trained in Boston, Massachusetts. He founded Iora Health[28], which transformed primary care in the US by moving away from the prevalent fee for service model to focus on keeping people healthy. He explains that it has been very difficult to get access to the data they need, he says, not because of technical limitations, but because of 'data hoarding' and organisations wanting to keep the data to themselves for competitive reasons (even though the data should really belong to the patient).

With the amount of unstructured data (for example, free text fields within EHRs or medical correspondence such as discharge letters or clinic letters) in digital systems, it is difficult to analyse data at scale. Furthermore, different health organisations capture the same data element in different ways – even a simple metric such as blood pressure could be recorded differently, requiring significant efforts 'harmonising' data before it can be aggregated in a meaningful manner.

Mark's team at Duke's developed a risk scoring system for patients at high risk of end stage renal disease, who could then be referred to a nephrologist for review[29]. The pilot conducted in 2015 cost $217,000 (60% for design and development of the application and 11% for data analysis and pipeline development). Given the differences in the data models across the various EHR, the team estimated that it would cost another provider $90,000 to validate the data pipeline and clinical workflow – a cost that could be up to $39 million across the 432 health systems in the US!

The quality of the data is affected by paper documentation and unstructured data inherently lacks quality control methods. Second, are the challenges frontline clinicians face when entering data into a system. A review of the usability of ED EHR systems in England in 2019 revealed that none of the systems reached the median usability score aligned to the industry standard of acceptable usability[30]. Third, when 'harmonising' data from disparate sources, this inevitably is based on a series of assumptions.

Bias

Bias can be due to underlying issues in the data or methodology. For example, a study showed that the algorithm the US healthcare system was discriminating against black patients[31]. This was happening because the algorithm used the cost of healthcare as a proxy for health need, and since less is spent on black patients compared to white patients with the same levels of need. It foregrounds an important requirement of AI in healthcare, which is to ensure fairness, that decisions or recommendations made should not discriminate against patients based on their demographic or other features.

Another common issue relates to training datasets: training data may not adequately represent the full range of scenarios, or include a sample representative of the population to which the model is then applied (for example, ethnic minorities underrepresented).

Accidental or unknown confounders can also impact the outcome of the model[32]. For example, if the algorithm is more likely to classify a skin lesion as malignant if there is a ruler in the image, or in identifying hip fractures if the x-ray was marked 'urgent'.

Generalisability

Generalisability refers to the applicability of a study to other contexts. With AI in healthcare, it refers to the extent to which a model trained and developed in one setting, country or (sub)population can be run effectively and safely in another context. Low generalisability significantly impairs the scalability of a solution.

Generalisability is tricky, for several reasons. There remains the possibility of biased data or reporting. There are operating and technical differences between various healthcare systems: countries have different thresholds and best practice guidelines, which means a model trained in one country may not work 'out of the box' in another. Validation issues could apply even within the same country and health system, even where there are no other 'obvious' differences. This is driven by the desire of many healthcare organisations to test out solutions themselves (and there should certainly be an extent of checks carried out).

External validation – testing of the model against appropriate datasets beyond that contained within the training dataset – can help develop generalisable models. However, a review of 516 studies of algorithms analysing medical images to provide diagnosis decisions found that only 6% did any external validation[33]. Even of that 6%, none of the studies incorporated design features required for robust external validation.

Accuracy

AI models sometimes have low accuracy and this could be related to several reasons mentioned above, including narrow focus and bias. While being slightly inaccurate when recommending what clothes a user may like is fine (annoying, but no harm done), getting it wrong when trying to identify cancer in a patient is not okay. With much higher stakes, and sometimes perceived rather than objectively worse performance (similarly to assessing the safety of autonomous driving vehicles compared to human drivers), AI in healthcare has a much higher 'entry bar'.

An added level of complexity is that mere 'accuracy' statistics, such as area under the curve (AUC) – an aggregate measurement of the performance of a classification model – does not give a clear indication as to whether it should be used in clinical practice[34]. How do you compare specify and sensitivity measures for an AI solution to the old diagnostic tests to determine which one works 'best'?

Consider accuracy in the context of explainability. While it may not always be a direct trade-off, which is more important and why? One study used citizen juries (representative samples of the public who are briefed on background to gain informed judgement on policy questions) to explore trade-offs between explainability and accuracy of AI solutions in healthcare (stroke and kidney transplants) and non-healthcare scenarios (criminal justice and recruitment)[35]. In the healthcare scenarios, an overwhelming majority (86% for stroke and 92% for kidney transplantation) voted for a system that focused more on accuracy rather than explainability (in contrast to non-healthcare scenarios where they favoured explanation more or both equally). In favouring accuracy in the healthcare scenarios, jurors considered the impact on the patient (saving lives in patients) whereas in recruitment they didn't necessarily feel there was one 'best person for the job'.

Unethical actors: cybersecurity, hacking and manipulation

Healthcare data is highly valuable, providing deep and personal insights. Unfortunately, this also makes it a great target for unscrupulous individuals looking to exploit or sell on the data. The Department of Health and Human Services' Office for Civil Rights showed 686 data breaches in the US in 2021 (up from 642 the year before)[36]. These data breaches equated to almost 45 million patient records being exposed or stolen. 74% of these breaches were due to hacking and IT incidents, using methods such as ransomware.

With AI, fundamentally powered by data, large amounts of sensitive data is potentially stored in the cloud and 'flow' between different systems. This increases the risk of unauthorised access.

Furthermore, AI itself can be used to manipulate health data unethically. For example, researchers from Israel demonstrated how Generative Adversarial Networks (GANs) – a form of deep learning that uses two 'competing' neural networks to generate new content – can be used to alter CT and MRI scans (for example, add or remove 'evidence' of cancer) to commit insurance fraud or even cause the patient harm[37].

Did Covid-19 help create AI success?

With an increased focus on digital and health tech during the pandemic, there must be several effective and scalable AI solutions out there? Not quite.

There were certainly some positives.

From a non-AI perspective, a team of researchers in Oxford UK developed the QCovid risk assessment tool for predicting the risk of Covid-19 related death or hospital admission[38]. The tool was validated to perform well and was used in February 2021 to add a further 1.5m patients to the shielded patient list (patients at higher risk of developing Covid-19 complications and advised to take additional precautions) and to help prioritise vaccinations for these patients. Later in 2021, the group developed and validated two further iterations of the algorithm – to identify clinical risk factors for unvaccinated patients (QCovid2) and vaccinated patients (QCovid3).

From an AI perspective, there were some successes in the pharmaceutical space. For example, BenevolentAI used NLP and relationship extraction algorithms to identify potential candidates from already approved drugs[39]. The company very quickly identified the previously unknown antiviral properties of baricitinib, a drug used for the treatment of rheumatoid arthritis. Following independent verification and a study that showed a 71% reduction in mortality in elderly patients with Covid-19, the drug was granted FDA emergency use authorisation.

However, the verdict on the wider application of AI models for Covid-19 was devastatingly negative.

There was a lot of effort put into identifying whether machine learning could help manage Covid-19 patients and related healthcare services. Laure Wynants, an epidemiologist from the Netherlands, said 'If there's any time that AI could prove its usefulness, it's now...

I had my hopes up.'[40]. She and colleagues published a paper reviewing models diagnosing, predicting prognosis and identifying patients at risk of developing Covid-19[41]. They reviewed 232 models (1118 diagnostic models, 107 prognostic models and 7 for identifying patients at risk of developing Covid-19) and did not recommend any for widespread clinical use. Only two models (one diagnostic and one prognostic) were identified with potential that warranted further validation. All models had a high or unclear risk of bias with many not including a description of the target population and only 46 conducting external validation.

The above findings were in line with a study published by researchers from the University of Cambridge[42]. They did a systematic review of 62 studies that were published in 2020 on machine learning models predicting the diagnosis or prognosis of Covid-19 from CXR and computer tomography (CT) scans. The review found that none of the models were fit for clinical use, based on issues with methodology (including poor quality data, joining different datasets together and poor application of ML techniques) or bias (data subsets that are not reproducible, inappropriate control groups, datasets that are too small and overlap between training and validation data). The researchers offered useful recommendations to overcome some of the challenges.

First, avoid joining up datasets and using data from public repositories (high risk of bias and low resolution or compressed datasets causing issues for ML models), and focus on matching demographics across cohorts. Second, carefully consider the validation dataset of appropriate size and with no overlaps. Third, pay attention to clear referencing of source data or code (especially when in public domain and being updated), assess research against established frameworks for reporting prediction models and explain pre-processing steps (for example, image resizing) in detail.

Both of the above reviews highlight the opportunity to improve things through collaboration between those who build solutions when it comes to gathering data, developing and validating models. This will certainly help sharing of lessons learnt, promoting best practices and reduced duplication of effort through the sharing of outputs.

CHAPTER 6

KEY THEMES WITH AI
IN HEALTHCARE

Sometimes, AI or data is not the answer at all. A large amount of resources are wasted on projects which don't target the problem, and the expected outcomes are most often not achieved. Even if outcomes are (partially) met, it is very hard to scale a solution beyond a single or a small number of organisations.

When discussing the potential for AI in healthcare, Dr Tom Foley doesn't see AI making a significant broad-based impact in the immediate future. Tom sees more opportunities in operational and 'behind the scenes' applications. In the near future, he believes, opportunities for AI will be dwarfed by the opportunities of simply applying 'basic' software engineering and data analytics to solve healthcare problems.

Tom illustrates the point with an example from an economic scale perspective. Everyone talks about healthcare being an enormous industry or market, accounting for 10% or more of the economy, and it is. But because current AI tools do interesting things in really narrow areas, the potential market or clinical impact for each is really a percentage of a percentage of a percentage. In contrast, when considering the back office procedures required in every industry, the potential user base is much larger, so it's easier to build things, get them right and to refine them.

Dr Vishnu Chandrabalan is the Associate Clinical Information Officer for Data Science and a consultant General Surgeon at the Lancashire Teaching Hospitals NHS Foundation Trust in England. He responds to the point that AI is not suitable in every situation with the following – a good surgeon knows how to operate, a better surgeon knows when to operate and the best surgeons know when not to operate.

AI IS NOT JUST ABOUT TECHNOLOGY

Successful integration

We need to stop thinking of AI (and data) as an answer in itself; a silver bullet. It is not that. It is a technology-based enabler; a tool that forms part of a wider solution and one that needs to be considered carefully in the overall design, along with non-technological factors that determine the success of an implementation.

Sundeep Khanna explains that this is not unique to healthcare and that in his experience, too many times it becomes 'all about the technology', with an approach of just 'plugging it in'. He says that change is often not managed effectively and that the workforce often do not understand their new roles and what the new processes need to be. He suggests that organisations need to be more accountable to their workforce and do more to provide information on the new technologies and their implications (he mentions a time where robotic process automation was discussed and the workforce thought this would be a robot sitting at a desk), especially with AI where there is more of a fear factor with implications for jobs.

Successful integration into existing clinical workflows and healthcare operations is a good indicator for success. Yosef explains his approach to developing workflows together with Happitech's partners, which was based on the principle that the solution should only alert patients and clinicians when they will be required to take action. For example, alerting when a patient who has not previously had a diagnosis of atrial fibrillation (AF) goes into atrial fibrillation and needs urgent medical attention, not when a known AF patient has AF again (in which a less urgent message advising a medical review may be sent).

Yosef explains the importance of identifying the right at-risk patients. At Happitech they worked in collaboration with the medical community, including cardiologists and GPs, to identify criteria on how to screen and who to screen so as not to add a burden to the system. It is important to follow clinical guidelines and do screening in a responsible way which doesn't create unnecessary demand and pressure based on no scientific evidence. He explains that for example, if you screen people in their 40s and 50s, where there is a low prevalence, that you will end up with a lot of false positives. He highlights this as irresponsible tech, which sends patients unnecessarily to a doctor. A recent US study, looking at data from EHRs and Apple Watches to identify users that would most likely benefit from anticoagulation if AF was diagnosed, proved this point[1]. The study shows that there is limited benefit, with only 0.25% of this user group identified with AF shown to be candidates for anticoagulation treatment. This study and Yosef's explanation above illustrates the wider point about weighing up the pros and cons of screening. While there can be significant benefits to screening programmes, screening is not always the answer, with incorrect results and unnecessary demands put on the healthcare system. It has been suggested that treatment of the disease or awareness to encourage patients to seek appropriate medical attention could be more effective[2].

Prashant Warier, CEO of Qure.ai, explains that he is a data scientist by training, and he has been working with data for 20 years. He did his PhD in the US in operations research, looking at optimising trucking networks. Following a stint in the retail sector, working on demand forecasting and price optimisation, he moved back to India where he worked with data to understand user behaviours and how best to target adverts. An innovative technology he developed was acquired by Fractal Analytics, which he joined as Chief Data Scientist. It was at Fractal where Prashant got the idea for Qure.ai, which was then spun out as a separate company.

Prashant Warier believes companies fail because they do not figure out the go-to-market aspect, and instead think 'this is all cool technology' and that somebody will buy it. The reality is, he says, that unless you figure out how to make it within a hospital setting, no one will want to buy it. Prashant explains that a successful solution needs to integrate with a hospital software ecosystem (which is often different from hospital to hospital) and be available to the clinicians who need to review it.

Let's go back to the point around narrow focus and AI being good at solving a very specific problem.

Professor David Lowe is a consultant in Emergency Medicine based at the Queen Elizabeth Hospital in Glasgow. He is also an honorary professor, with a MD focused decision making in high acuity situations and a Master's in human factors and simulation. David is currently working on a number of projects looking to integrate ML into clinical contexts, working with both commercial and academic partners. He warns about the safety aspects associated with edge cases and the considerations for testing to support implementation. David explains with an example on reading chest x-rays, human radiologists don't just look for a specific abnormality like ML solutions do, they look out for any abnormality across all areas of the chest x-ray.

David Higgins is a former academic turned life sciences entrepreneur (making the transition from neuroscience to AI), who works with funding agencies and investors in an early stage CTO-as-a-service role. Since 2017, he has split his time between academia and the healthtech industry. David has founded two venture funded start-ups, one in pharma R&D and one delivering behavioural change therapy to patients, and is a visiting researcher at the Berlin Institute of Health. From June 2022, he is also working with German Entrepreneurship, an organisation fully funded by German taxpayers, to setup an 'AI competence centre' based in Berlin to help start-ups in the use of AI.

He has an interesting take on how companies can approach the narrow focus problem. He observes that most companies go 'wide' first, for example, focusing on diabetes as a whole. His advice is to first pick a niche that you can do really well in, and then to go to neighbouring illnesses; then expand a niche in a sustainable way.

One way to address narrow focus is to foster collaboration, and develop platforms and provide incentives that bring together solutions that complement each other and together, presenting a more holistic solution akin to that provided by a human clinician.

AI is not an 'island'

AI is not self-sufficient and it cannot function by itself. Yes, AI models can perform beautifully on a fancy computer in a lab or the trendy offices of a start-up. Release it into the 'wild' and the data is messy, healthcare professionals have strong opinions and patient safety comes first.

One of the key complexities is around the machine-human interaction, which is an even more important element with AI than with non-AI based health technologies.

Dr Terence Tan is the global medical director for Ubie, a Japanese company founded in 2017 and working on clinical AI products in the areas of productivity, workflows, and symptom checkers. He observes the relative ease of developing AI based on analysing radiological images: the radiographer or radiologist is tech savvy, because they operate within the most digitised speciality in healthcare. He points to an element of development bias when it comes to certain healthcare personnel, for example allied health care professionals (physiotherapists and occupational therapists) or nurses who currently operate in very non-digitised and manual work environments. Terence stresses the importance of addressing this bias, as these groups form a significant proportion of the healthcare delivery system. A related point is ensuring the right balance when engaging with healthcare professionals. For example, senior doctors and nurses will have more clinical experience as well policy and management experience. On the flip side, more junior doctors and nurses may have more relevant 'workflow' and systems insights as they are working more of the 'doing' on the ground.

This engagement with healthcare professionals reinforces a point Chalinda Abeykoon makes on the importance of founders understanding the base levels of tech adoption in an industry when developing and launching solutions.

The right 'mix' in a team helps. Yosef Safi Harb attributes a great mix – a strong medical team and those with technical backgrounds (aerospace, signal processing, computer vision.) – to the success of Happitech.

Dr Mark Sendak makes a similar point regarding the success of the Innovation team at Duke's, 10 highly talented individuals and a range of skills from clinicians, business consulting, to full time data scientists and data engineers. He highlights the importance of having leadership buy-in; the team reports directly to the CEO of the health system.

This applies equally to academics working on research projects. Elizabeth Dolan[1], a third year PhD candidate at The Horizon Centre for Doctoral Training at the University of Nottingham, is working on a PhD exploring the use of non-traditional data and AI techniques in predicting diseases and their spread (more on this later). She highlights the challenges of translating research into real life application – for example, research may come up with a brilliant prediction but if it doesn't help healthcare professionals make decisions in a clinical setting, it's effectively useless. She emphasises the importance of

---

1   Elizabeth Dolan is supported by the Horizon Centre for Doctoral Training at the University of Nottingham (UKRI Grant No. EP/S023305/1) and by the University of Bristol external partner.

researchers engaging earlier on with healthcare professionals, and also the importance of using mixed methods in research. For example, as well as the quantitative methods, using qualitative methods such as interviews with patients and healthcare professionals, and getting them involved in the design.

Dr Tom Foley and Dr Vishnu Chandrabalan both make an additional interesting point. They stress the importance of 'translators' in the middle, people who understand both the technical and clinical (and operational) elements.

During a career break, Vishnu taught himself a variety of technical skills and develop a number of projects on Amazon Web Services (AWS) exploring NLP, crypto markets, financial markets and, of course, healthcare. He feels that the technical skills he has acquired, combined with his clinical expertise, allows him to act as a 'Rosetta Stone' between technologist and clinicians (for example, when considering AI solutions vendors to bring to the hospital), sitting between, and understanding, and translating.

Another key element is integration with other hospital systems. AI solutions need to 'talk to' and 'work within' systems that gather and store patient information (for example, EHRs) and information about investigations and results (for example, PACS and radiology information systems or RIS).

Integration with hospital systems is important for access to, and continuing access to data. It also makes for easier incorporation into existing clinical workflows, resulting in a better user experience for healthcare staff in terms of limiting the number of different systems to use and reducing duplication of data entry efforts.

Emma Selby explains the plans at Wysa for taking this important step and integrating it with the electronic patient record. When an individual wants to use Wysa, they will get a text message which allows the creation of a secure link. This link enables information to flow back into their medical record where clinicians can see the outcome measures and progress.

ACCEPTING THE LIMITATIONS OF AI

Dr Victoria Betton is a social worker by qualification, and she has always been interested in innovation and in how big institutions and bureaucracies work. After corporate roles in the NHS, she moved into digital through her PhD on digital media and how it affects mental health. While working at the Leeds and York Partnership NHS Foundation Trust, she convinced commissioners to fund £100,000 to explore the potential of digital health. As she started to experiment and codify her approach, other hospitals started asking her for help. She subsequently set up mHabitat as a trading arm of the NHS Trust to help organisations use digital innovation for social impact and address real world problems.

Technology is one part of it, she says, but 'How do you make it work in practice?' With AI, there are many other elements to consider, she says, from creating a value proposition to being compliant with regulation before you can start thinking about prospectively validating a solution. She warns that it is easy to get caught in what technology and data can do, without asking, 'Have we got something useful to people?'

A significant limiting factor to AI adoption is an NHS organisation's ability to adopt and implement AI tools, Victoria says. She refers to her experience of working with many healthcare organisations during the pandemic, and observes that they are extremely stretched, further reducing the time to invest in adopting AI technologies.

Dr Neil Paul is a GP in England, and passionate about technology from the age of eight. With computers at home as a boy, and involved in programming using languages such as Pascal, he considered pursuing computer science as a career, and suggests that he might have gone to a health tech start-up, had those existed in the same way at the time. After choosing to follow a career in medicine, his interest in computer science was reignited when he started in general practice. He illustrates the challenges facing a small AI start-up trying to get adoption of their product with a comparison. Neil explains that small companies often lack insight into how the NHS and primary care work. He points to a large pharmaceutical company trying to work with regional innovation agencies to promote a new lipid-lowering medication meant to significantly improve life expectancy. It had limited impact. 'If a pharmaceutical company with massive marketing budgets, established sales representatives, access to key opinion leaders, and experience doing this exact thing, had difficulty gaining adoption for a proven, evidence-based intervention, how can we expect the small AI start-up to do so?' Neil suggests that companies need access to on-the-ground advice – for example, a centrally funded clinical advisory panel. He also suggests that adopting innovation may need to be incentivised, similar to medicines management or other quality related initiatives which are incentivised with extra funding.

Vinod Khosla got it wrong. Machines will not replace 80% of doctors, and there is really no debate about that.

There are several reasons for this. I have already discussed the limitations associated with narrow focus. We also contend with the complexities of information and diagnosis processes within a healthcare setting. For example, the need to gather and consider information from a variety of sources including relatives and the high incidence of 'non-perfect' information which requires an element of 'judgement' to interpret correctly. There are the 'non-technical' elements of delivering healthcare – the empathy that is required considering non-medical challenges patients and families face, and the non-verbal cues that are important to consider during interactions.

The real question is how AI can enhance the care a professional delivers. Whether it's doing the boring stuff that healthcare professionals hate doing (and AI can do better), helping them make more informed decisions or helping them perform a task more accurately, there are plenty of opportunities for AI to add real value.

Healthcare professionals spent a large amount of time on administrative tasks. A study of 4,720 US physicians revealed that the average doctor spent 16.6% of their working hours on administration[3]. This time varied by clinical speciality with the three specialities spending the highest time on administrative tasks being psychiatry (20.3%), internists (17.3% and general practitioners (17.3%).

Alex Kafetz believes that we should always leave the power with doctors and that AI is a tool to make the best use of their time and reduce administrative task time. A big sports fan, Alex refers to the decision review system (DRS) used in cricket. Technology is used to aid the umpires make the correct decisions. The technology doesn't make autonomous decisions or say that the umpire is wrong. It says, 'Here is some new evidence, what would you like to do? Would you like to change the decision?'

From another non-healthcare perspective, Sundeep Khanna points out that the fear about job security arises from a lack of understanding, and that there needs to be an educational effort to address this. He says that when people fully understand that it can make their job better and that AI is never going to be able to do certain elements of their job, it makes it easier. They almost see it as their personal assistant, 'that never calls in sick and never complains about their manager!' Sundeep also points out the organisation is accountable for explaining what and why they are considering AI solutions, and to get people involved in the conversations early.

A good example of the complementary nature and scope to integrate AI into clinical workflows is a 2016 study which explored the application of deep learning techniques to identify breast cancer[4]. Results indicated that when the solution's predictions were combined with the human pathologist, the accuracy increased and the human error rate decreased (from 3% to less than 1%). The deep learning system on its own was less accurate than the human pathologist. While more recent studies have shown increased accuracy of AI models compared to humans, this early study illustrates the important point of how AI can enhance rather than replace humans.

Dr Kiruba Nagaratnam highlights that the experience level of the clinician also makes a difference to the level of engagement and perceived benefit. Discussing the Alberta stroke programme early CT score (ASPECTS) for stroke and the Brainomix solution, he explains that the most experienced clinicians may have a view that they 'do this all the time' and therefore they can still do a better job than the machine, so they will do the score themselves rather than rely on the new software. The less experienced clinicians who didn't do the scoring previously are more likely to rely on the score they are given.

Clíodhna Ní Ghuidhir works as the Principal Scientific Advisor for National Institute for Health and Care Excellence (NICE). She leads delivery of a multi-agency advisory service for data-driven tech, which provides guidance, advice, and information on the regulatory and evaluation pathway for health and social care. Her NHS career began on the Management Training Scheme where she worked as a service manager before moving into policy at NHS England & Improvement.

Clíodhna Ní Ghuidhir provides a tip for when working with the NHS, be more upfront about the uncertainties and how hard you are working to resolve them, rather than do a slick sales presentation. She suggests rather than just saying 'It was trained on a diverse population' to 'take the time to show how you've analysed the training examples and how you've analysed the population to whom you ultimately want this to apply to'. For example, if it's data from an epidemiological source like the UK Biobank, to state 'what we know about epidemiological collected samples compared with the actual patient population sample... Or to plan further studies that will bottom out any uncertainties'.

She also suggests that risk aversion is partly driven by imprecise risk articulation. By asking 'Why?' when something goes wrong and when it's not performing as expected, she says we can really dig into specific causes. Clíodhna suggests that more precise and very proactive risk articulation by developers and improved risk literacy could support more widespread acceptance and adoption of AI in healthcare.

Validating results can be tricky

Vishnu stresses the importance of taking an evidence-based approach. He reminds us that as a trained clinician, you wouldn't 'try' a new operating procedure or a new drug on a patient without robust published, peer reviewed literature.

He elaborates that there are only two circumstances in which you could do that without the full evidence: as part of a phase three clinical trial, or within a research context and under very controlled circumstances.

Vishnu explains that one of the practical difficulties of validation (and reproducible research) within the NHS healthcare context is that each organisation structures data in their own way. Therefore, if a solution was developed in one organisation, it can't be easily validated on another organisation's data. He is leading the mapping of his hospital's data to the OMOP data model standards[5] and on to a common data warehouse. If all or most organisations map their data on to a common model, then it would enable more collaboration, and reduce the amount of repetitive work and duplication.

However, it's not that easy. Organisations are not completely free to choose the standards and how the data is structured; they may be limited by their vendors and contracts. As Maxine highlighted, there are also many standards and no 'one' standard that has been mandated centrally. Should there be more 'enforcement' and 'disincentives' to move to a single data model? On a pragmatic level, Vishnu also points out that a single standard can be mandated for grant funding, for example for any funding through Health Data Research UK (HDR UK).

Professor David Lowe stresses the importance of the methodology with which the validation study was designed. What is the gold standard, for example in ground truthing, is it at pixel level or with contextual clinical information? What is the evidence we require before we can start using it demonstrating both clinical safety, acceptability, and sustained engagement? Are the patient clinical or economic outcomes being evaluated through a randomised controlled trial (RCT)? Or is it a stepped wedge design, where all clusters are exposed to the intervention rather than half with a RCT and more clusters are exposed to the intervention later in the study, more appropriate?[6] Cost of evaluation can be high and creating frameworks that enable competitor analysis between potential vendors to support procurement decisions will be critical.

On discussing the ideal context to most closely mimic real life when conducting validations, David explains that at a national level if they were to procure a stroke solution to identify patients suitable for thrombectomy, they would want to test all available solutions against the same dataset. Furthermore, that dataset should be constructed to reflect the natural distribution rather than a specific subset of images from a specific hospital or tertiary centres, taking into account factors such as scanner type and clinical acceptability due to workforce variation.

Dominic Cushnan is the Head of AI medical imaging at the NHS AI Lab where he works to figure out mechanisms and levers to support the complete journey, from creation of AI models right through to how the models get deployed back into the clinical pathway safely. Before healthcare, he ran a technology company focused on computer vision technologies and human interface technologies, working on projects across various industries including defence and pharmaceuticals. After working with leading technologies on various projects, he got interested in matters beyond technology after reading a paper about delivering change in complex environments. During the pandemic, Dominic set up the National Covid Chest Imaging Database (NCCID).

With respect to validation, the 'right' type of validation and doing it in a way that minimises the need for individual organisations to 'revalidate', Dominic agreed that everyone was generating evidence in a slightly different way and there was no clear plan as to how to standardise evidence generation. He pointed out that imaging, at a more advanced stage with AI, is the burning platform on which to have these standardisation conversations.

Moving towards cultural acceptance

Ming Tang is the Chief Data and Analytics Officer at NHS England and NHS Improvement. She believes that we are much more likely to use data in an innovative way post Covid-19, and be more proactive and predictive in our analyses. She explains that because we have experienced access to more data and decision support analysis, people have higher expectations for more timely data.

Nuria Oliver's experience supporting the Covid-19 response in the Valencian Region of Spain have led her to similar conclusions. She explains that before the pandemic there was a cultural challenge; the public administration in general didn't have a digital mindset yet, and were not really data driven. The pandemic was a catalyser, helping the administrators realise the value of data to support decision making and accelerating the required digital transformation.

Nuria also highlights the strong and timely response her team got from the public via the citizen survey, which fed into the model supporting the decision making. The survey was designed to help understand how the public was doing, and what impact the pandemic was having on their lives. It also gathered information on how many people were wearing a mask and how many were supportive of vaccinations.

The survey got more than 140,000 responses in the first 48 hours of launching on 28 March 2020. She explains that it was very emotional, a grassroots movement, where everyone pitched in to help spread the word through universities, associations, social media, email, and WhatsApp. She believes that so many people responded because the survey gave them a voice. The aggregated analysis and visualisation of key elements is available online at https://ellisalicante.org/en/covid19impactsurvey

A study analysing more than 150,000 responses in the week that followed revealed useful insights[7]. As well as (perhaps expected) findings related to differences in social behaviours across age groups and genders, economic impact on small businesses and negative correlation between economic damage and willingness to self-isolate, it also revealed that 28% lacked necessary resources to properly self-isolate and that only 1% of the population was tested. A model, developed to identify variables correlated with a positive test result, accurately predicted the prevalence of Covid-19 at 5%.

A CAUTIONARY TALE: IBM WATSON HEALTH

IBM Watson progressed from humble beginnings as a 'question and answer' solution, beating two 'Jeopardy!' champions in a televised game in 2011. Soon after, IBM identified healthcare as a key industry to target and by 2012 had two pilots, one with Wellpoint, a large US insurer), and one with Memorial Sloan Kettering Cancer Center[8].

Wellpoint wanted to focus on utilisation management, and make the review process of approving provider requests for procedures based on health plans more efficient. Memorial Sloan Kettering wanted to personalise cancer treatment based on patient genetic information.

Watson Health evolved into a collection of products applying various ML techniques. IBM invested more than $4 billion to make acquisitions to gain access to medical data it needed and created Watson Health in 2015[9].

It then suffered a number of high profile failures.

The most high profile was in 2013 at Houston's MD Anderson Cancer Center, and designed to help oncologists make clinical decisions. The hospital team published a paper in 2018 admitting that the solution, Oncology Expert Advisor, had varying degrees of success[10]. For example, while it had accuracy up to 96% in diagnoses, it only had a maximum of 65% when it came to therapy timelines.

A Wall Street Journal investigation published in August 2018 is reported to have stated that more than 12 partners and clients had stopped or reduced Watson oncology projects due to limited impact on patients[11]. Watson couldn't keep up with fast evolving treatment guidelines, it said, and despite more than $15 billion investment there was no published research on positive impact on patient outcomes.

After spending more than $60m, MD Anderson Cancer Center stopped the project citing 'multiple examples of unsafe and incorrect treatment recommendations'[12].

Why did the project fail?

Firstly, there appears to have been a lot of hype around the success of 'Jeopardy!' and almost a naive approach choosing to tackle cancer, a highly complex specialty with a variety of evolving information sources to consider.

Jeff Cribbs, a research vice president at Gartner, explains that there were genuine AI innovations in NLP and other areas such as knowledge extraction, but that 'the hype got ahead of the engineering, as the hype cycle says it almost always will, and some of those struggles became apparent'.

Martin Kohn, a former chief medical scientist at IBM Research, is reported to have said that he remembered advising Watson be used for very specific tasks such as predicting adverse reactions to drugs rather than recommending cancer treatments[13]. He was told 'he didn't understand'.

In line with 'garbage in, garbage out', the quality of the training was criticised. David Howard, Professor of Health Policy and Management at Emory University explains that Watson simply didn't have enough high quality published research available to analyse, with not many studies having randomised controlled trials[11]. It was also hard for the solution to accurately 'read' medical records due to acronyms, human errors, shorthand phrases, and different styles of writing[14].

Further, clinicians did not trust the system. Clinicians had to input data into the system and predictions were based on the data entered by Memorial Sloan Kettering clinicians rather than wider research. The solution was designed to learn from clinician input and clinicians were empowered to enter their own recommendations, based on experience, and not always based on evidence[14]. Dr Mark Kris, Memorial Sloan Kettering's lead Watson trainer, explains that it's hard to keep up-to-date, for example when treatment guidelines for lung cancer change, because they have to enter all the related research and case studies. Essentially, they relied on the expertise of clinicians from this one hospital, which led to concerns of bias and non-compatibility with guidelines outside of the US.

Costs and the administrative burden were high. The solution costs between \$200 and \$1,000 per patient with additional consulting and EHR integration costs[14]. If not linked with EHRs, a lot of time needs to be spent manually entering patient information.

IBM was reported to be trying to sell off the Watson Health business in early 2021 and it later completed a sale to Francisco Partners, a global investment firm[15].

CHAPTER 7

STRIVING FOR GOOD PRACTICE WITH AI

As I reflected on the main challenges and themes emerging, I began to identify a number of key features and questions to consider when designing, developing, and implementing AI in healthcare.

VALUE AND OPPORTUNITIES

What is the (perceived) value?

It is very important that all stakeholders clearly understand what benefits that the solution can deliver (and that it can be clearly explained). Is it realistic? Can it be made to work in the 'wild'? Does it take into the harsh realities of delivering care on the frontline, and can you point to or count the benefits it delivers, or helps to deliver? Or does it make life harder for healthcare professionals? Does it create more work for healthcare professionals or for the healthcare system?

Professor David Lowe highlights that the value proposition differs for each stakeholder group. For clinicians, managers, and patients with its impact on clinical workflow, it's about integration, safety, regulatory approval and cost. For the end user, it's about engagement, improved clinical and patient outcomes.

Yosef refers back to his journey with Happitech and reflects that showcasing the savings is really hard and that you need a high number of patients (users) to prove benefits. He explains that it's 'chicken and egg' when hospitals ask for evidence on savings, but you are early-stage: you need adoption and patients to be able to demonstrate benefits. Yosef says they were lucky to have had great hospital and technology partners that helped them such as OLVG Hospital and Luscii, and visionary doctors that really believed in the product, who were really supportive and co-created the solution with the Happitech team. In this way, he explains, the supporters can see, first-hand, the progress, feedback from users and how it improves outcomes. This helps, but Yosef reports that they still needed to convince insurance companies and other stakeholders, and had to manage each hospital asking the same questions and wanting to prove it themselves. He says that once they got to a certain 'tipping' point, that it was easier to provide evidence and get exponential growth.

Ming Tang shares a collaborative approach her team have been pursuing to identify where ML can best add value to existing healthcare data. Ming is in the process of setting up clinical review groups, with appropriate clinical governance, to provide an effective forum for discussion and review of clinical data to identify trends and opportunities for improvement. For example, the NHS is aiming to identify variations in clinical pathways and outcomes, and to focus on opportunities to improve cancer care, which has suffered during Covid-19. She thinks this approach would be helpful to encourage discussion and generate curiosity, and move from admiring the data visualisation to 'What do I do with it?'; to providing insights and discussion on what should and could be done differently.

Vishnu talks about a similar initiative he is leading. He is working on collating and sharing the metadata (references and information about the characteristics of the data) related to the data at the hospital, and sharing that with the healthcare professionals at the organisation. Vishnu is asking them 'Can you go and think of ideas as to how you can use this data?' He recognises that this is not specific to AI, that it opens up possibilities and gets people thinking. For example, most didn't realise that they have been collecting vital signs of patients for the last four years.

Gary McAllister is the Chief Technology Officer for OneLondon, a partnership of the NHS and local government across London working to join up health and care across the region. He is responsible for ensuring that the technology across London meets the architectural standards for the NHS and best practice. Gary was one of the leaders who developed the London care record, which brings together all the information from primary care, secondary care, social care, mental health across the region. He explains that the expectation is that they use data across London for research and direct care, service improvement and for commercial use. As part of his role, he meets with key operational and technology leaders across London weekly to discuss current topics, emerging trends and strategies, and policy or funding opportunities.

Gary gives an example of identifying value in the context of the biggest operational challenges. Backlogs for elective surgical procedures and medical reviews are at an all-time high. There is scope for a more nuanced approach to tackling the problem, he says, rather than simply taking a 'start at the top or bottom' approach. This is more about taking an intelligent approach to the referrals that feed the waiting list. He explains that most of the current 'non-urgent' referrals are 'anonymous' in that it's hard to differentiate from other referrals, and to not take a 'first in, first out' approach. Gary points out that eight out of ten patients seen in outpatients are discharged without further intervention. For patients with symptoms related to the heart or the chest, 'What if we can prescribe a device that can be worn in the community, that enables monitoring and if indicators fall outside certain thresholds, they can automatically be referred in for specialist review?'

Karen Johnson says that as a Director of Finance, she is happy to support any programme that has positive outputs for the patients and is financially sustainable. The key, for her, is to be able to articulate and quantify the benefits, which is sometimes very difficult to do. Many solutions are implemented, showing real benefits around patient care through improved processes, which saves nursing time – but this doesn't drive direct financial benefits with the safety requirements around nursing ratios. One of the key barriers to benefits realisation is an accurate baseline or starting point. For example, when a solution is expected to deliver 10% efficiency, 10% of what? Karen explains that she wants to be able to refer to a baseline, agree the expected benefits (10% of efficiency against the baseline) and sign off the project based on the agreement that it delivers against these benefits, which they will measure progress on.

Karen's Hospital has changed the focus of its Project Management Office (PMO) function from the traditional cost centre to improving value, reducing duplication and reducing inefficiencies which in turn will drive productivity and improve financial sustainability. As we emerge from the Covid-19 pandemic, where financial efficiency wasn't the top priority, she observes that measuring and realising expected benefits will become more important as we move back to the reality where public funding will ultimately have to be managed within set limits.

Funding mechanisms to match the need

No one individual or company can make AI successful in healthcare. What is needed is an environment where adequate resources are available to support adoption and funding mechanisms are in place. Further, a regulatory framework which provides assurance on patient safety in a pragmatic way before, during and after implementation.

Funding mechanisms and flows are a key component that needs to be addressed at system level.

Reimbursements for AI solutions is still a very new area, not surprising given that reimbursement for digital health interventions are also still in a very immature state. Yosef explains that for Happitech, together with their hospital and remote patient monitoring partner Luscii , they were first to get the national healthcare authority in the Netherlands to provide them with a targeted reimbursement code.

When asked about the US market, where reimbursements for digital health solutions are more mature, he explained that the US reimbursements are based on the devices and that if you have a novel device that you might not fit into the code structure. He further explained that a lot of the digital health applications have to be assessed on a case by case basis since there are no direct comparators. Yosef emphasises the importance of developing varied business models – for example, partnerships with MedTech, pharmaceuticals hospitals, and thinking about who you are providing value to – as it could be years before you get to reimbursement codes.

Grant funding is another means of supporting innovative AI solutions to develop and gain adoption.

Daniel Bamford is the Deputy Director of the NHSX AI awards, running the programme, and he explains that in addition to being a grant process, it provides individualised, innovation pathway navigation and problem solving support to the award winners through assigned relationship managers. This support could cover regulation, information governance, trial design or reimbursement, and also provides the award winners with a more efficient channel through which to engage with the wider NHS stakeholders.

Daniel explains that the funded technologies have benefited over 100,000 patients up to March 2022, and by the end of March 2023, Daniel expects the number to exceed 200,000. He notes that certain clinical pathways have moved faster to adopt AI-based solutions, for example he estimates that approximately 70% of stroke units in England have an AI solution embedded in the pathway. Daniel explains that this is due to the award 'pump priming' broader clinical and operational transformation on the pathway, for example, the updates to the national stroke specification published this year.

The award will have three rounds of applications, evaluations and funding and Daniel considers this as three waves of companies they support as they go through their journey developing their evidence base and establishing a route to the NHS market. He explains that the late stage companies from the first round of funding are now at that stage where the team are having conversations about commissioning, and supporting making the case where the policy landscape needs to change.

Dominic Cushnan points to health economics as another key area feeding into reimbursement models. He says the question 'Do AI diagnostics actually save money?' is still being debated. Dominic explains that there is a misconception that these are a 'one off' cost, that once you buy it, it sits on a shelf and just works. Factors to consider when identifying whole life costs include, he notes, ongoing engineering support, licensing costs, cloud storage and computational power.

Daniel explains that his team has created an expert evaluation advisory group consisting of international academic experts and representation from NICE, MHRA and clinicians. They have been able to support the design of trials that meet NHS evidence requirements and cover key elements such as accuracy, safety, effectiveness, value, implementation and feasibility and sustainability of scaling up. There is a paper due to be published highlighting the insights gained from doing 15 of these large multi-year evaluations.

Using AI to overcome bias

We have discussed how poorly curated datasets and incomplete methodologies can cause bias and result in health inequalities, but AI can actually help overcome bias. Maxine Mackintosh describes a study where black patients were reporting higher degrees of pain that couldn't be explained by the findings on their x-rays. That led to situations where these patients felt that their symptoms were not being taken seriously and they blamed for being 'too sensitive'. When a deep learning model reviewed the x-rays, they found new, objective features within the x-rays that correlated with the amount of pain black patients articulated[1].

Multimodal data presents exciting opportunities

With the rise of wearables, social media and digitisation of many industries, the number and variety of data sources has increased significantly.

One of the key types of data that has significant value is text data where one of the challenges is that it is often stored in an unstructured form, making extraction, and analysing more complex.

Dr Jonny Pearson is the Lead Data Scientist in the NHS Transformation Directorate Analytics Unit. He supports the need for efficient reproducibility from a different perspective. He sees, within the NHS, an analytical mindset when approaching data questions – get the answer, as needed, now. We need to move to more of a developer mindset where we can set up processes and methodologies that can enable another person to use the same or similar data. This will then enable more sharing and collaboration.

Jonny is aware that text data gets missed, sometimes, in data strategies, and that over the next few years, we need to focus on getting the enablers that will allow maximising the insights we can get from text data. He explains the value of multi-model datasets, for example combining medical image data with text from related reports, enabling more context and matching up of patient outcomes with activities and inputs. He makes a further point that we need to consider how we view and explore data: graph-based tables, where connecting 'nodes' makes it easier to identify patterns, can be more informative than tables with rows of data.

Elizabeth Dolan started her career in events management after completing a degree in English. After taking a break to raise a family, she retrained in computer science specialising in using predictive analytics in information systems within the energy sector. She was exploring information from smart metres, Internet of things (IoT) and the grid, aggregating information to create energy assets and identifying structures that will help renewable energy. It was then she saw the potential of using data from digital footprints. This led her to her PhD, where she is focusing on how shopping data in England – loyalty card data and transactional shopping data from retailer at aggregate population level – can be used to help diagnose disease and improve healthcare.

Initially, she explored was whether it is acceptable for people to donate that data. 'What might they be worried about?' 'What are the ethics to consider?' 'If people are happy for the data to be used, can we do something useful with it?' In interviews with 40 people, Elizabeth found the response to be really enthusiastic. The shopping data was already in public use and they were happy for it to be used. The acceptability went up as she explained and people understood exactly how the data would be used. Interestingly, acceptance was also linked to convenience – people wanted it to be easy to 'donate'. For example, Tesco developed a new function on their website which allows users to send Clubcard data to a third party, which is what Elizabeth is using.

The first use case Elizabeth is exploring is whether shopping data can provide insights into symptoms related to ovarian cancer, leading to earlier diagnosis (ovarian cancer typically presents very late due to the non-specific nature of the symptoms). Early results are very interesting. Women who were advised by the GP to self-medicate were shopping significantly more, and that they were seven times more likely to wait over a year for an accurate diagnosis. In the future, these findings may warrant an introduction of a safety net, ensuring that women advised to self-medicate are followed up within a certain time period.

The second use case was highlighted through the Covid-19 and was around whether aggregated (non-person level) shopping data from retailers on items used to self-treat respiratory conditions (for example, cough medicine and decongestant medicines) could predict patterns and spread of infectious diseases (such as Covid-19). Elizabeth thinks that this approach could potentially be a useful tool for surveillance purposes.

It is possible to develop a system to acquire and aggregate all of the potentially interesting data, perhaps hosted by an independent body such as the Wellcome Trust (an independent global charitable foundation supporting research to solve the urgent health challenges) in a biobank, but, Elizabeth says, doing so would require significant amounts of effort and investment. Therefore, clear value needs to be demonstrated in the types of data. It would also be sensible to explore where existing data acquisition, collation and storage processes and infrastructure can be reused. Elizabeth also points out that with GDPR, people have a legal right to their digital footprints and can request it from companies, making the (theoretical) process easier.

DATA, INFRASTRUCTURE, AND IMPLEMENTATION

Access to training data is a challenge in healthcare, with high levels of regulation and ethical considerations, especially if you are a start-up. Access is only one issue, because once you get access, the quality of the dataset is often debatable.

Gary McAllister agrees that data quality is a significant issue. Thinking back to when he was involved in setting up genomic medicine centres across England, he recalls that the data quality was very poor and identifying cohorts to develop suitable algorithms was very challenging.

When combining cohorts together, he says, it leads to a lot of false positives (for example, prediction of having a disease when actually they do not). For example, during the shared care record programme, when putting application programming interface (API) layers to enable access to the data they had, it led to a lot of false positives due to incorrectly captured or classified data.

Gary explains that plans are underway at a regional level, across London, to develop a data platform, first understanding what data types need to be bought together and then collating, classifying, and cleaning up data quality issues.

What could have a big positive impact? Gary suggests creating an open algorithm platform for the NHS, with appropriate image viewers within it, that would allow algorithms to be openly shared and incorporated into clinical pathways. This would foster a collaborative and learning culture, that will progress the AI ecosystem beyond the pockets of innovation that it is currently limited to.

Ming is leading on an initiative that changes the way the NHS uses data. This work is focused on collecting the data at source, by putting in data pipelines to extract the data rather than rely on data collection that relies on each trust to extract and codify data en masse based on standard schemas or templates. She explains that this programme aims to reduce burden on the data supplier, and because data is being collected based on specified use case, it is more specific and doesn't rely on codification prior to submission, which often creates a lag and variation in data quality depending on the capability of Trusts to process data prior to submission. Gathering at source associated with a workflow provides more complete data and forces discipline to enable better understanding of which elements of the data are actually useful and which elements are just noise.

Professor James Teo is Professor of Neurology and Clinical Director for data and AI at the King's College Hospital NHS Foundation Trust in London, and he agrees with the importance of collecting and using data at source. He also believes that data is not 'the new oil.' James explains that oil is non-renewable, largely fungible (almost identical regardless of site of extraction and) and primary use is after processing away from the site of extraction. In contrast, he explains that healthcare data is renewable and non-fungible as it contains properties and context of the source it derives from. Removing this metadata reduces useful dimensionality and may introduce bias, therefore data is most useful processed and analysed at the collecting site. James believes this leads to a more vertically integrated model, so a significant proportion of AI development needs to be decentralised even if using centralised foundational models.

Maxine highlights the effort and cost of clearing up and preprocessing data for use in AI. She cites an example from when she served on the DeepMind Independent Review Board: DeepMind spent £8m getting the Royal Free hospital data ready for research. She makes the point that AI can be useful in this scenario, to support the cleaning of data and identify best ways to manage missing data.

The importance of enabling infrastructure

Enabling infrastructure is a requirement for successful AI adoption.

This is the case even in the more digitally mature healthcare organisations. Vishnu explains that at his hospital sites, they are digitally mature and have a EHR for 15 years. With two main clinical sites, they are nearly paperless at one site. However, this data has historically been used for retrospective business intelligence, not for any data science or AI applications exploring predictive use cases.

His attention is on what he is calling 'data discovery', to identify where all the data is and to prepare a data catalogue or data dictionary.

A related initiative is creating reproducible data pipelines. He illustrates this with an example. If an analysis was done on ovarian cancer data and the data is pulled into a bunch of CSV (Comma Separated Values, a file format in Microsoft Excel) files and sent off, and then when someone comes back to say, 'That's great, now can you do the same for colorectal cancer?', it takes six months. That shouldn't be the case. It should be a matter of adjusting the ICD-10 codes to change the diagnosis and we should be able to reproduce the analysis very quickly.

Harshana Liyanage is the Lead Data Scientist at the UK Health Security Agency (UKHSA). After an undergraduate degree in computer science and 7 years in the software industry, he completed a PhD in computer science. Harshana then worked as a postdoctoral researcher in health informatics, gradually focusing on epidemiological and health data analysis. He says that 'having the complementary technical experience from a programming point of view and the logical background from academic work' helped to redefine himself as a data scientist.

At the UKHSA, he supports surveillance outbreak investigations and the health protection teams working regionally by developing technical solutions for surveillance and routine reporting. Harshana says that they are focusing on maximising the potential of analytics, for example interactive web based reports, before thinking about incorporating complex AI solutions. He explains that they are implementing best practices such as Reproducible Analytical Pipelines (RAP), which automate and standardise how data is analysed, to improve the quality and enable scalability. They are using modern software engineering best practices, he reports, such as open source development and continuous integration-continuous development (CI/CD) deployment.

Harshana advocates for 'standard ways of working' to enhance collaborative development, resulting in the rapid deployment of public health solutions.

Another initiative Vishnu is developing is a trusted analytics and research environment which uses multiple cloud-based services for providing a secure, collaborative environment for data science. Working with various universities, the environment uses open technology standards and common data models to make available numerous structured and unstructured datasets. The platform will have two clusters – one that's internal, and one that's public facing, and containing no patient data.

Professor David Lowe emphasises the importance of interoperability, and not being limited to a certain vendor's predictive model, which may have been trained and tested in a different country, or a patient cohort very different to the local population: the concept of AI drift and the importance of post market surveillance to ensure that device continues to conform to technical and performance characteristics. This comes back to more guidance from the centre in terms of standard validation requirements and, potentially, common datasets for validation.

Both David and Dominic also highlight the need for a 'deployment' infrastructure to enable choice for the end user on which model to use, how it is integrated into the clinical workflow and other systems, and how the data is presented. David gives the example of PACS and RIS which have an integration platform layer that allows users to select from multiple different vendors, a prostate cancer or lung cancer nodule solution. Cost is a consideration, as vendors increasingly move to cloud based solutions and transacting large volumes of data across the internet. This raises issues around information governance and contracting as patient identifiable data shared with vendors.

A staged approach to implementation

Before AI can deliver these benefits, certain enablers need to be in place: legitimate access to data on an ongoing basis, and data of sufficient quality (it may need to be transformed appropriately before use).

Equally, the underlying processes and clinical workflows must be in place, in a reasonable state to support integration of AI or to be automated (and we should not automate broken processes, these need to be redesigned first). Maxine Mackintosh points out that often we are good at overlaying computational statistics and automating not very effective systems. Adding more layers of complexity often leads to frustration because it amplifies inaccurate inputs and shaky foundations. There is little point in making something that doesn't work very well more computational or automated.

A roadmap is needed, to plan what is required and its order. A roadmap also helps check whether activities you thought were completed earlier have in fact been completed.

'How do you manage the people that are going to be most impacted by the AI solution?' 'How do you manage senior stakeholders?' 'How do you manage end users including consumers or patients?' 'What needs to change to support the success of the AI solution and is it feasible?' 'How do you maximise benefits realisation and how do you deal with time it frees up?' These questions are a good reminder, Sundeep Khanna says, that it's not all about the technology, and there is a need to consider a holistic approach. He knows the importance of helping people develop a roadmap, (from strategic objectives all the way through to execution via scaling up pilots), and that an operating model covering people, processes and technology is essential to driving successful adoption and transformation.

Matt Bourne is the CTO and Director at Tiny Medical Apps, where they have developed the Digital Health Passport which enables young patients in England to upload and share Personalised Asthma Action Plans, supporting self-management and reducing emergency admissions to hospital. The solution includes educational resources, weather alerts (for example, pollen count) and medication reminders.

Matt's team realised that the NHS in England was not going to be ready for AI at scale for a while, and they must take a five year staged approach to AI with their solution. Level 1 is a product that is standalone, not connected to any NHS systems and available for patients to download for free. This stage includes a level of customisation, so if, for example, a healthcare region wants to include local public health campaigns or signpost patients to local asthma services, they can.

Level 2 includes a degree of interoperability, taking a very pragmatic approach. It could be summarising key information and pushing that into the GP systems in primary care (and this may be 'synced' only at selected times, for example, ahead of an annual asthma review). Level 3 builds on the integration to more closely support a clinical pathway to provide information when it is needed, and to the various healthcare professionals that need it.

Level 4 moves on to risk stratification, where it's more personalised, taking into account factors such as not taking medication. Matt doesn't see this stage using ML either. Level 5 is where he sees ML playing a key role, for example in helping predict asthma attacks over the next six weeks.

Dr Murray Ellender, a practising GP and CEO at eConsult, which supports digital triage and remote consultations in the primary care setting in England, describes a similar approach, building on a strong non-AI foundation before bringing in AI. Murray has always been interested in technology and joined the innovative GP surgery at Hurley in 2006, where he co-developed eConsult to meet the internal demand to make triage more efficient. Requests from other GP surgeries led to establishing eConsult as a commercial enterprise. Demand for the service skyrocketed during Covid-19, doubling the number of GP surgeries from 1,500 to 3,000 within the first six weeks, and from 120,000 consultations a month to 1.2m a month. Using the solution allows GP surgeries to 'centralise' the processing of these triages to a group of clinicians who become very efficient at the task.

Murray explains that he has consciously not built in any AI yet, because the clinicians make the decisions and that he wants to take clinicians along the journey with him. They have gathered a large amount of data, structured questions related to different questions and related to the outcomes. This, coupled with grant funding won through the NHS AI in Health and Care Award, provides a perfect platform to start bringing AI in. Murray sees opportunity to take measured steps. For example, flag to clinicians that every time this type of patient is referred to a pharmacy, 'Would you like us to do that automatically for you'? Then gradually build up trust and accuracy to get to the stage where the referral happens automatically and does not need approval by the clinician, where appropriate.

Governance and transparency

Alex Kafetz believes that it is important to have mature conversations with the public, to tell them that AI will mean they are 'interacting with health professionals in a different way' and 'might even get less time with them' but 'more quality time'.

He also highlights an interesting point around the perceived 'enemy' in the public eye. Alex explains that five years ago, pharmaceutical companies would have been seen as the enemy, focused on making money. Of course, things have changed since the pandemic with the pharmaceutical companies developing life changing vaccines, and AstraZeneca and Pfizer becoming part of everyday conversation. He further explains that the "enemy' focus has now shifted to Big Tech - Google, Facebook, etc and about having meaningful conversations about access to data, why it's important and doing it safely.

Yosef details the approach they took to build trust when collecting data at Happitech. There was absolutely no need for personal data: they didn't need to know who you were, what you did, or your address. They adopted a privacy by design methodology, so the data they collected was compliant with GDPR (and this was independently verified by Deloitte). They also communicated why they were collecting data, what they were using it for, and who they are sharing it with. The support of the Dutch Heart Foundation was really important to get the message across.

Data privacy and information governance

This is a topic closely related to trust.

Barry Moult is a nurse by training and started as a full-time Data Protection Officer (DPO) in England in 2003. He has a refreshingly pragmatic approach to data privacy. Someone asked him, 'Where will we be without AI in 10 year's time?' This made Barry realise that it's not going to be 10 years, but much sooner, maybe even just two years away. He thinks that if we want to deliver healthcare efficiently and cost effectively, that we need to do things differently and that AI can help. He is a big supporter of AI, 'as long as it's done properly'.

An involving and crucial subject is data ownership. Barry illustrates this with an example where an organisation came to him with a solution to help high intensity users of healthcare services. There were three phases – one to build the algorithm, second to test the algorithm and third was ongoing support. From the initial stage, the company wanted to be a joint controller of the data. Barry explains when the company is building an algorithm, they need access to data, but will not be deciding what happens to the data. They are data processors, operating within the confines of what the healthcare organisation instructs and authorities. In the third stage, when they are going to run the algorithm but also provide support and training for people to be able to interpret insights and take action, only then do they become joint controllers.

Barry explains that the key consideration when providing access to data (and potentially sharing data) appropriately is the review of risks. Data Protection Impact Assessments (DPIA) are a tool to identify, assess and manage risks appropriately. One key factor is the level of anonymisation of the data – completely anonymised, pseudonymised (personally identifiable data is replaced but can potentially be replaced by someone with the right data) or not anonymised at all. The other key factor is the level of transparency. 'Do the patients know their rights to opting out?' and 'Do the patients' understand what their data is being used for?' The other key element is related to GDPR and whether there is a lawful basis for processing that data – which could be anything from contractual, consent from the patient or legitimate interest.

One of the challenges we face is the variance between healthcare organisations, and the approach they take to information governance and data privacy. Barry acknowledges this, and that a more unified approach across the NHS, even if a simple template, would be helpful. He suggests another useful exercise might be to bring together 10 to 15 experienced information governance professionals from across healthcare for a workshop to work through the commonly encountered scenarios, converting the benefits, pros, and cons of each. At the end of the workshop, to come up with guidance and templates, which will provide a 'central' view on risks and potential mitigations (which each local organisation can then review and decide how they want to proceed).

An essential aspect with AI is monitoring after implementation, to ensure that it still works (and to facilitate continual improvement) and is safe to use for that particular scenario in the context of changing environments, clinical guidelines and of course the data itself. This presents additional challenges from an information governance perspective. Barry highlights the real concerns around what is really happening to data at this stage. He explains that while agreements can help, independent monitoring may be needed to ensure correct usage and sharing.

Barry advises that the key thing is to get information governance and data privacy teams involved at the beginning of the project, so that compliance can be built into the design and implementation.

Can you explain how it works?

Transparency is really important for acceptance, Ming confirms. She explains the approach they took while creating a bed demand forecasting tool during Covid-19 to predict the number of people that would need hospitalisation and type of hospitalisation e.g. ICU usage and oxygen requirements. The solution was built taking information from various sources including the national Covid-19 Test and Trace programme and Google Mobility data. Transparency was provided through insights into which inputs into the model was driving the predictions, which gave the team a way to understand the model and using that to engage with clinicians and the people that were managing the response to the pandemic.

Dr Mark Sendak recognises that 'when you train in and practice medicine, sometimes you need to trust things that you don't totally understand'. 'This is why people say medicine is an art and a science'. He refers to lithium (a popular mood stabilising drug in the treatment of psychiatric conditions such as bipolar disorder, depression, or mania), where doctors trust that it works, although the exact mechanisms of how it works is not known. 'We may not understand entirely how it works, but we do it because it mostly works.' Dr Michael George agrees and highlights that if a doctor does something based on gut feeling, how can we expect AI to be able to explain everything? He explains the challenge of the 'right to explanation' element set out in the GDPR guidance which means decisions made by AI models will be required to offer an explanation. He further points out that sometimes we do trust technology without an explanation, for example when using Google Maps for driving but that in the context of healthcare (or in other high-stakes contexts where a decision could negatively affect the subject), most would demand an explanation.

Talking about accountability

As AI in healthcare become more advanced and more widespread, it becomes increasingly important to identify and mitigate issues regarding accountability.

Dr Terence Tan reflects on the fact that as healthcare professionals, they are responsible for acts of commission and acts of omission. For example, if one amputates the wrong leg, that would be rightly liable. One would also be liable if they didn't operate in time. Terence explains that he thinks the broader conversation should be around liability and responsibility. For example, if a manufacturer produces an intravenous line with a fault in it that admits air, then a degree of liability sits with the manufacturer rather than the nurse that used the faulty line.

Several options have been proposed in the US context[2]. The first option is that an AI solution can be considered a 'person' and therefore can be sued directly for negligence. This would necessitate that the AI solution be insured against such claims. The second option is to introduce 'common enterprise liability' which will hold all groups involved in the implementation and use of the solution liable. The third option is to adjust the role and responsibilities of healthcare professionals requiring them to exercise due care, which includes evaluating the black box AI technologies, and therefore assigning them the liability. This is difficult for reasons discussed already around skills and complexities regarding accuracy and the various related metrics.

While options are fully explored and implemented across different legal jurisdictions, which will take time, the most pragmatic approach needs to be followed. For example, Dr Kiruba Nagaratnam explains that with the Brainomix software, while the system provided an output, it was the clinician's decision (and therefore, their ultimate responsibility) as to how they used it and that the human radiologists report is the final verdict that went into the patient record.

Maneesh Juneja reports that people often say to him 'I don't want any algorithms in cars and I don't want computers in cars making decisions for me'. To which, he points out that 'when you're driving a car with an automatic gearbox, the car is deciding when to change gear up or down... The same with the airbags'. He notes that 'you have already ceded some control because the car is going to decide when to deploy the airbags in the event of a crash. It's not you, as a human driver, completely in control of driving the car'. In healthcare, there is automation, he says, whether it is with clinical decision support systems or in the operating theatre, and we must be realistic – even today healthcare delivery is not fully under human control.

Working collaboratively

Fostering collaboration enables sharing of ideas, best practice and reduces waste and potential errors such as the ones that occurred during development of Covid-19 models.

Giuseppe Sollazzo is the Deputy Director at the NHS AI lab and the Head of AI Skunkworks & Deployment, which supports early adoption of AI in healthcare by providing free short term expertise and resources. He has always worked in technology, he says, and he jokes that he was one of those people that could code before he could write. Family members in medicine created an environment that got him interested in healthcare, and he worked for a software company that developed systems for hospital laboratories. Part of his purpose, he says, is to share knowledge and build a community to bring people together. He hopes this will bring hospitals together to talk to each other about their work, and that this approach will improve AI in healthcare over time, and allow compilation of common problems and solutions that worked.

Arfah Farooq is an expert community builder. She co-founded Muslamic Makers, a Muslim- in-tech community that came about from her own experience of working in the tech field and not seeing herself being represented in events and not seeing role models who look like her. She connected with an acquaintance from a similar background on Twitter, and after chatting, they put on their first event, which was attended by 50 people. Now they have over 1,000 people on their Slack channel. What started off as an informal event and Slack channel is growing into a fully fledged not-for profit, and they recently secured grant funding to support a tech scholarship programme. This experience led her to pursue a career in community building, and she worked as the community lead for the NHS AI Labs.

At the NHS Transformation Directorate (formerly NHSX), her role sat within the AI Skunkworks programme, which helps people in the system experiment with AI tools. Arfah explains that while a lot of organisations in the NHS and the way they do things are different, a lot of the problems they face are the same. She gives an example of a project she was involved with helping Gloucestershire Hospitals NHS Foundation Trust develop a solution that would accurately predict the risk of a patient staying longer than 21 days (long stayers) when admitted to hospital. This is not a problem only faced by Gloucestershire Hospitals NHS Foundation Trust, and having released the code on GitHub, the team was grappling with how to get the code into the hands of the community and how they could get other hospitals to start implementing it, too.

Arfah explained that she created engagement through webinars, discussions and workshops, and now another hospital, Nottingham, has taken up the code and the Skunkworks team is helping them use that code to experiment in their own environment.

It is not just about what they do centrally, she says, it's also about learning from the community. They may be working on their own projects and their own initiatives, and the platform they create centrally should allow them to share their work, so other people can learn from it.

Collaborative approaches are now being developed more widely. Dr Mark Sendak has been discussing with colleagues how they could work at policy level to address barriers to diffusion of innovation, and how sites with lower resources can access and implement innovative solutions. They have identified capacity building as a crucial first step. This echoes Gary McAllister's analysis that one of the challenges to full potential realisation of the Global Digital Exemplar (GDE) programme, where hospitals lead on digital adoption received funding, was that smaller hospitals did not have the same digital capabilities seen at the larger GDE sites. Mark explains that if we can start to standardise, develop best practice and train the teams to conduct procurement, integration and lifecycle management, this will improve how AI is adopted and used across healthcare settings in the US. He highlights that this will be the focus of the new Health AI Partnership launched between Duke, Mayo Clinic and UC Berkeley and law firm DLA Piper.

What compromises collaboration?

First, and as previously discussed in the context of reproducible research, is the disparate data models. Maxine Mackintosh points out that standardisation is an important requirement for collaboration and consists of two elements: standards for data, and robust operating procedures.

Then it is about people. Maxine highlights that shared values are really important. Vishnu explains that the infrastructure and security required to share and collaborate exists. However, the reason why sharing doesn't happen often relates to the people involved. Dr Vajira Dissanayake is a medical geneticist by background and a pioneer in shaping digital health and related clinical education in Sri Lanka. He is currently the chairman of Commonwealth Health Professions and Partners Alliance, and Commonwealth Centre for Digital Health, President of the Sri Lanka Medical Council and Dean of the Faculty of Medicine at the University of Colombo in Sri Lanka. He recalls instances during his tenure as the president of the Asia Pacific Association for Medical Informatics where he was pushing for sharing of knowledge and algorithms across the region to create a central resource and democratise the whole thing. However, it never materialised because no one wanted to share anything. Everybody feels like there is intellectual property and sees a commercial opportunity in what they're doing.

The incentives to collaborate are relevant. Dominic Cushnan led the development of the National Covid Chest Imaging Database (NCCID) during Covid-19. This was a centralised database containing medical images (x-rays, MRIs and CTs) from across the UK, created to support the development of technology that can improve the delivery of care for Covid-19 patients. Dominic explains that during the pandemic organisations such as NHS England were allocated special powers to collect, process and share confidential patient information they needed to manage Covid-19 and deliver patient care, and that all hospitals were required to share data into the NCCID. He highlights that not all hospitals shared their data. He recognises that one issue is technology; it is not as easy as clicking on a button to share the data into the centre. The second issue that Dominic sees is around incentivisation and payment for staff time. For example, if a hospital was approached by a multinational technology organisation asking for access to their data for research purposes and they were going to pay for it (and potentially offer equity in the venture), hospitals may be more likely to allocate time to these ventures.

The next evolution of collaboration could be 'open collaboration'.

Bart De Witte is the founder and CEO of the Hippo AI Foundation, which is a charitable data trust for data altruism which focuses on facilitating and supporting communities to accelerate the open-source development of medical AI. Bart explains how he drew inspiration for the need for equal access from an episode of *Altered Carbon* on

Netflix. The show portrays a futuristic society with flying cars and the downloading of consciousnesses from a person into another body. He was struck by the fact that even in this incredibly advanced society, an individual needing emergency medical treatment was denied because they did not have enough insurance credits. He cites examples of open source which really helped progress science and created value, including the internet being based on open technologies such as http and the Covid-19 genome being sequences and shared quickly.

Bart believes that we should not create (artificial) scarcity around data and algorithms, and that the next stage in terms of value creation could be when innovators compete on creating the best experience or brand. This will require a significant shift in mindset where we have to be comfortable with making the underlying data available as well as the source code. Bart has been working on a licence that facilitates this, providing free access, with the condition that anything created needs to be shared in the same way. He reiterates that just because it's open (and you don't 'own' it) doesn't mean you can't monetise it, and that you can still charge for a product or service. He closed a partnership with AstraZeneca where they are going to open up their breast cancer data to his initiative and also financing the related work at Hippo AI. He believes that all commercial companies that handle patient related data need to take such an approach as it will lower their R&D costs. This of course only works when all companies share. To solve this, Bart has been working on ESG certificates that are connected to a metric that calculates the impact of the data sharing and donations.

Does open source and open data work in theory? Giuseppe Sollazzo's Skunkworks programme is based on an open source model, where suppliers taking part sign up to these principles. Giuseppe explains that, while of course some suppliers have expressed concerns about intellectual property, it hasn't stopped any of the projects going ahead. He sees it as a business opportunity for the suppliers. Indeed, it would provide many of them a great opportunity to work closely with a NHS organisation, gain experience with NHS datasets and to develop a relationship to continue working with the organisation beyond the Skunkworks programme.

Education and training

Successful adoption of AI requires a skilled workforce across various disciplines including clinical, technical, digital and operational.

Dr Vishnu Chandrabalan believes that we need a new breed of clinicians, that medical and nursing schools include data science and AI as part of the curriculum, to better operate and contribute to a future environment where AI will be much more prevalent. He explains that they need to know what AI is, what benefits it can deliver and what the risks are.

Dr Vajira Dissanayake agrees that the impact of technology is only going to increase and raises the question as to what future medical students and doctors need to be like to help effectively. Vajira shares some photos about a new facility that is being constructed that will house a dedicated area to showcase the digital transformation and systems that are ongoing across the country in order to promote education and engagement. Dean of the Faculty of Medicine at the University of Colombo, Vajira suggests that AI and digital health technology be embedded in undergraduate education.

Professor David Lowe gives a practical example of the need for clinicians to have a better understanding of this subject. A clinical decision support tool might have been approved through the FDA or have received the CE marking based on having a certain sensitivity and specificity level. 'Do all of the front line clinicians fully understand the implications (and therefore, limitations) of the sensitivity and specificity? Especially if they are tired and it's 2am?' AI solutions often require well calibrated clinicians that can incorporate AI insight into often a Bayesian approach to decision making. In many clinical contexts staff may be challenged to do this, with a requirement for significant training and support. Dr Kiruba Nagaratnam agrees with the importance of clinicians having a base level of understanding of this. During the roll out of e-Stroke, he emphasised the importance of setting expectations of what it can and can't do, and then providing training, and to include the limitations of the system.

On the technical side, we need to focus on the data analysts. Dr Jonny Pearson believes this is an area that can be professionalised. He explains this is being able to scale up the workforce in a systematic way to provide a right mix of skills within the analytical workforce. Data analysts are classed as admin staff in the NHS, Jonny says, and that there isn't a clearly defined career progression for them. The key point is 'not to replace the workforce with new people but to enable the current workforce in a way that emphasises both analytical knowledge and training'. This leads to a workforce with increased technical skills and one that feels empowered to provide evidence based analysis to support decision making across the system.

He emphasises the need for people who have been in healthcare and understand it, as well as people who have formal data science training to bring a more 'developer' mindset and best practice on validation, bias and other technical aspects of developing models.

In the context of GDEs not realising full potential, with the lack of digital skills in smaller hospitals, Gary suggests that a 'build it and they will come' model does not really work and that funding needs to go to organisations that are the worst performers, with a bolstered set of expertise and leadership to help them realise the benefits of the funding. These more 'general' technologies and digital skills are essential to support and complement the data analyst skills.

In all of the above instances, clearly defined career paths with the appropriate balance of 'from health' and 'from outside' personnel who will help standardise and scale out the capability while providing communities of practice to support collaboration and learning.

From an 'operational' perspective, it is essential to consider the knock on effects of successful AI implementation in healthcare. If AI reduces or removes the need for an individual to perform 'lower level' tasks within a role, this will free up time allowing them to take on more complex (or different tasks). Another example is AI that provides 'real time' support during delivery of care which means that clinicians can maximise the level at which they can operate safely and effectively. Careful planning must be undertaken to ensure that the individuals in these or other such scenarios are supported and to maximise opportunities to deploy resources optimally to mitigate workforce shortages. For successful implementation, we must collate the knowledge required to develop best practices and make available training and informal support to upskill the individuals.

CHAPTER 8

A ROADMAP FOR THE PRACTITIONER

After an exploration of the success stories, the challenges, and good practice with AI across industries, it is time to think about how to 'bring it together' into a single methodology that will help those who are looking to develop, fund, procure or use AI solutions in healthcare.

My intention for this book was to distil insights from across academia, practitioners and those gained from talking with more than 40 experts into a guide to help you, and to provide a 'system' level view for those looking to make sure the best possible supportive environment exists.

EXISTING RESOURCES ARE PIECES OF THE PUZZLE

There are many great publications and frameworks that are relevant. I'll introduce existing resources in three distinct areas:

1. General technology implementation
2. AI implementation
3. Reading for further understanding

Please do familiarise yourself with them, while keeping an open mind about the intended purpose and scope of each. I expect you to find they suit your situation in part and not entirely, for reasons I will be elaborating on shortly.

General technology implementation

The first type of resource is that exploring the implementation and adoption of technology generally within healthcare. One of the key points here is that technology is only one part of the puzzle. Nothing describes this better than Professor Trish Greenhalgh's non-adoption, abandonment, scale-up, spread, and sustainability (NASSS) framework[1].

The study identified key domains through a systematic review and then reviewed six technology enabled healthcare programmes – including video consultations and remote monitoring – using longitudinal ethnography and action research for up to three years to develop the domains further.

The framework describes the following seven key domains (where technology is only one domain):

1. Condition
2. Technology
3. Value proposition
4. Adopters (healthcare professionals and patients)
5. Organisation
6. Wider system (for example, societal)
7. Embedding and adaptation over time (also considering interactions between domains)

Each of the domains have questions, for example, within the technology domain considerations include the types of data generated and the knowledge needed to use the solution. Other questions cover key themes that we have discussed – regulatory and socio-cultural elements (within 'Wider system'), readiness, funding decisions, extent of change and work required to implement (within 'Organisation') and the impact on the role and identities of healthcare professionals (within 'Adopters'). There is a dedicated domain on value proposition, exploring both supplier and receiver perspectives.

Domain seven raises the important point that there is linkage between the domains and during a programme, and that these can evolve, for example due to various policy or other changes (for example, unprecedented events such as Covid-19). One of the questions within the domain 'Scope for adaptation over time' identifies the importance of being able to adapt the technology and overall solution. They also highlight difficulties adapting staff roles and services where these were subcontracted, sometimes to private companies. It also raises the point more generally about the type of relationship with the solution supplier, whether it is 'transactional' or more of a 'partnership' with collaborative working and a common objective(s).

The researchers identified a number of challenges through the case studies explored and classified them as either simple, complicated, or complex. Programmes with multiple complex challenges rarely became mainstream.

AI implementation

The second type of resource is that specifically exploring the implementation of AI within healthcare.

David Higgins and a colleague developed a framework, based on a three phase approach, that proposes key activities for stakeholders including founders and investors that are required to take a biomedical solution from conception/incubation to market[2]. The activities are focused around four areas: clinical validation, regulatory affairs, data strategy, and algorithmic development.

Phase one, *Form*, is focused on assembling the (multidisciplinary) team to develop a solution to address a clinical need. As well as exploring technical feasibility, the team needs to understand clinical validation and regulatory requirements in taking the solution to market. The key output of this phase is a proof of concept, although one where the need has been validated and it is more than a 'model developed in isolation on a computer'.

Phase two, *Build,* is focused on developing a basic solution that is broadly compliant from a clinical and regulatory point of view. The team from phase one evolves and works together over a period of 18 months to five years, with certain team members (such as the clinicians only working part time on the solution).

Phase three, *Launch,* is focused on completing the required clinical validation and regulatory activities (the bulk of which should have been completed in phase two) and gaining the appropriate certifications and evidence, to enable implementation of the solution in a clinical setting.

Throughout the three phases, risks, objectives, and key results are defined, and the authors provide advice on how to maximise success. For example, the importance of developing and testing the hypothesis related to market-fit early within phase one or making contact with regulatory bodies early on in phase two.

They also highlight an important aspect, which is often overlooked – the risks that need to be mitigated following the launch. Implementations don't just stop after launch, changes need to be made and compliance is required throughout operations. The authors point out the importance of planning for regular software updates to ensure any issues are fixed promptly and that risk to the patient is minimised (similar to aerospace or car industries). Changes may also be needed due to changes in clinical standards. Surveillance is required (similar to monitoring of adverse effects of medicines in the pharmaceutical industry) to quickly identify any unintended consequences of using the solution and also with certain AI techniques, a knock-on effect of the algorithm evolving with learning.

Clíodhna Ní Ghuidhir reports that with AI algorithms – which are contingent on the environment or data inputs, and therefore any changes can impact the algorithm's performance over time – it is really important to think about real world monitoring. She suggests that we could learn at what is already out there in this area and gives the example of surgical registries which monitor performance of surgical departments and surgeons and patient outcomes, because the context (in this case, individual characteristics of a patient) can be really important to surgical outcomes and registries capture this data.

David points outs that the product development roadmap following the launch phase (which will follow a shorter timeline due to already completed compliance related processes), aligning more those seen in non-regulated markets, with more focus on sales, scaling and developing new features.

Following his first paper above, David says the number one question people asked him was, 'How to follow a regulatory compliant development path?' In response, he published another paper which he describes as a 'technical person's how-to to regulatory for medical AI'[3]. This is based on the good machine learning practice (GMLP) guidelines and is a comprehensive resource I would recommend anyone interested in technical development of AI solutions in healthcare should read. The guidance covers the relevant aspect of the life cycle from data curation, model optimisation, consideration of 'adaptive AI' (As Clíodhna highlights above) through to post market planning.

Dr Sandeep Reddy is a medical doctor and academic with an avid interest in healthcare technology. After initially exploring the various elements of AI, he is now focused on the translational end. The Translational Evaluation of Healthcare AI (TEHAI) framework was developed with an international team over one and half years as a result of thinking about the lack of results in AI in healthcare following the hype, infrastructure development and funding being applied to the area. He describes the development of the framework as ongoing and organic linked to the medical and vendor community. Sandeep also explains a study (in the process of being published) of applying the framework retrospectively to screen and score over 900 Covid-19 studies, mainly related to imaging.

The TEHAI framework aims to fill the gap in functional, utility and ethical components of existing AI evaluation frameworks[4]. It was developed following a literature review, identification of further components considering technology evaluation and translation principles and ratified by a panel of international experts. TEHAI has three main components – capability, utility and adoption – and 15 subcomponents.

The Capability component focuses on the technical elements including dataset sources and integrity, and internal and external validation. The Utility component focuses on usability and applicability of the solution to a particular use case and to the domain, and includes elements such as safety, privacy, quality and generalisability. The Adoption component focuses on the factors required for successful adoption beyond technology, efficacy and safety, including elements such as integration with other technology systems, acceptance by healthcare professionals and patients, and benefits to the domain.

To help with the practical implementation, the authors highlight how the subcomponents should be checked based on the various stages of a programme. Three phases are described, although the phases are slightly different to the ones described by David Higgins – Development check (while the solution is being developed), Deployment check (during implementation) and Discernment check (ongoing monitoring). To provide further structure the authors propose a 0 to 3 scoring system for each subcomponent along with weights for each subcomponent.

Dr Mark Sendak and colleagues, in their case study about the development and implementation of Sepsis Watch, conceptualised as a socio-technical system requiring integration, highlight four key values and practices to support the development of clinical decision support solutions[5]. As discussed above, sepsis as a subject limited the options for model interpretability as a means to ensure transparency and therefore these four suggestions alternate options to achieve fairness, accountability, and transparency in machine learning (FATML) values.

First, is a clear definition of the problem, with adequate details that will be recognised by the healthcare professionals that will be using the solution. In this particular instance, the team had been involved in previous attempts and the healthcare professionals were involved in selecting the training cohort, elements included in the model and the design of the evaluation. The authors stress the importance of working with clinical stakeholders to understand elements of the clinical pathway that need to be included and also that the indicated use (and contraindications) of the solution needs to be clearly articulated (done using a 'Model fact' sheet in this instance).

Second, building trusted relationships with the various stakeholders (for example, clinical, technical, data, nurses using the system, and management responsible for resource allocation to support) by engaging early and regularly. These activities, and associated ones related to professional education, are resource intensive and in this instance a full time role was created to lead on this.

Third, is to respect the value of the healthcare professional and identify how to enhance their abilities (and not to replace them). For example, the Sepsis Watch tool was designed to be a diagnostic aid only with human clinicians making the final diagnostic decisions. AI solutions can also provide opportunities to develop new roles and capabilities. For example, the RRT nurses developed expertise in contextualising and synthesising digital patient data to remotely evaluate sepsis.

Fourth, is to ensure ongoing and multi-directional flow of information and feedback between the solution developers and the users. This could include various forms of meetings and workshops, as well as monitoring tools such as the monitor displaying Sepsis Watch model's behaviour in the developer's office. Another key stakeholder group is patients. As well as using ethical processes and existing care delivery pathways and personnel, where solutions interface more directly with patients, additional methods may be needed. Mark highlights that a 'community representative' such as within the Health AI Partnership can support this flow of information.

In a similar vein, Scott et al proposed a checklist of 10 questions clinicians can ask the developers of solutions[6]. The questions include probing around context (this might be the purpose of the algorithm, how does it complement existing clinical pathways, and can it be transferred to another clinical setting), and risks and benefits (for example, what was the quality of the training data, what is evidence for it improving patient outcomes and does the solution raise ethical or legal concerns).

We can't expect clinicians to take on the responsibility of vetting AI solutions without changes to resource allocation and the way we think about clinical career paths. I will discuss options for this later in the book.

Reading for further understanding

The third type of resource is more general.

The NHSX report Artificial Intelligence: How to get it right highlights research conducted by the Royal Society of Arts (RSA) in 2019 to better understand human factors associated with the spread of new and complex technology[7]. The research, to understand interactions with technology, barriers to adoption and potential solutions, included in-depth interviews with professionals developing, procurement and using data-driven technologies in the NHS. Recommendations included rigorous tests for bias, building momentum through first demonstrating benefits of back-end (non-clinical) solutions, upskilling the workforce and improving access to sandboxes (safe testing environments) to encourage innovation.

Another NHSX report, A buyer's guide to AI in health and care, offers practical advice for those involved in making decisions related to buying AI solutions in healthcare including senior manager, pro-curement leads, chief officers and clinicians[8]. Out of the various advice provided, four stand out and complement the ones discussed above.

First, it reinforces the all important question of 'what problem you are trying to solve'. The report provides additional insight into questions to ask about the availability of adequate amounts of data and whether it can be accessed ethically, and whether the model output will help solve problems in the real world (and whether the accuracy of the output can be tested). It also suggests that, depending on the answer to these questions, AI may not be the right answer.

Second, does the solution perform as the supplier claims? Does it do what it says on the tin? The report makes several important points. For example, trade-offs between sensitivity (accurately identifying actual cases) and specificity (accurately identifying negative cases) depending on the implications of missing a diagnosis versus over-diagnosing. It highlights the Area Under the Curve (AUC) is a helpful general metric reflective of model accuracy. However, it cautions of the limitations of the AUC due to its theoretical nature and being potentially misleading in cases where the underlying data is not evenly distributed. As pointed out in the report a 'confusion matrix' (comparing predicted with actual values) provides a way of deriving sensitivity, specificity, PPV (Positive Predictive Value is truly positive if the test is positive) and NPV (Negative Predictive Value is truly negative if the test is negative). David Higgins says that in his experience, all four of the measures are well understood in the clinical community. Finally, it highlights the need to compare models with the 'as-is', either solutions it replaces or processes (or humans) that it will enhance.

Third, is how and if the benefits claimed are translated into practice in the environment of the organisation. In terms of evidence, NICE has an Evidence Standards Framework for Digital Health Technologies, and if the solution is a medical device, clinical evaluation reports (CERs) provide clinical evidence. Further practical questions to ask include: What changes will your organisation need to make to realise benefits? Does it fit seamlessly into user workflows? Does it integrate with other technology systems? What data and other architecture requirements does the solutions have? How can you monitor whether the stated benefits are being realised?

Fourth, is how the product is managed and supported after implementation. This links to the post-launch risk mitigations flagged up in David Higgins' framework. The report adds further points: being clear about what your organisation's responsibilities are, and whether you have the capabilities, and what data the supplier expects to be sent back (and related approvals and information governance arrangements required).

Building on solid foundations

All of the above publications on frameworks, implementation, and the procurement and use of AI solutions converge on a number of common viewpoints.

Firstly, is the paramount importance of knowing what problem you are solving and that the solution you are proposing solves that problem (and that you can prove that it does).

Technology is definitely only part of it. To really understand, to have a successful implementation and wide adoption, a socio-technological lens is required considering the context within which a solution is deployed and various stakeholders that need to support it and work alongside it. It is a journey with several well defined stages from before the model is built, to building the model, deploying it and monitoring it afterwards.

I believe there are three main areas where the existing thinking can be developed further:

1. Each publication covers certain parts of the puzzle (and very well). Collating information from many different sources is a challenge and the reader can benefit from a single source offering a 'full view' of the approach to take and what wider facts to consider.

2. On a related note, existing resources focus on particular 'stages' of the journey. For the practitioner to successfully implement a solution they must understand the importance of every stage. This book considers and explores every stage, for example, it expands on those key activities that need to come before building the model and on monitoring (post-implementation) as a stage in the process.

   It is important to consider the time and activities 'between' the stages, whether you are following the approach below from start to finish and you have to wait a while to move to the next stage, or if you are 'starting' from a stage further along the journey. Before you (re)start, look at the stage before to ensure all key actions are complete and any risks that were identified are being managed. If you were previously following a different approach, carry forward any outstanding actions and risks, as well as 'look forward' to check you will not be missing anything by following the approach below.

3. Most approaches focus on one solution or one team level, 'What do I have to do to develop and deploy this successfully or what do I have to be aware of to buy and implement a solution?' This book also considers the system level, what needs to be in place and funded to create the enabling environment .

The approach I have developed attempts to provide a more holistic view. Although I consider the key aspects, I will not cover all the details (and wherever possible, I will point to other resources where the reader can access those insights). I will also bring to life some of the points with examples and insights from the experts and practitioners I have interviewed.

A NEW ALTERNATIVE

The proposed approach consists of a 'roadmap', laying out the key stages and activities from each of the main stakeholder group's perspective, and a list of enablers to support a successful implementation and subsequent adoption.

Three questions to ask yourself as you face the roadmap:

1. What problem are you trying to solve?
2. Who are you, and what stage are you or the solution in?
3. Which of the enablers are in place?

What problem are you trying to solve?

Before we explore the roadmap, there is a vital starting point. Furthermore, this question is one that needs to be revisited regularly throughout the approach.

What problem are you trying to solve?

A clear definition of the problem is needed, which then should be validated. This will lead to a better solution-problem fit.

AI is not always the answer and we should not start there. For example, Abraham Kaplan describes the 'law of the instrument' as the following[9]:

> Give a small boy a hammer, and he will find that everything he encounters needs pounding

We must be mindful that the optimal solution may not be AI based and may need something simpler.

Clíodhna Ní Ghuidhir points out that it all ultimately starts 'the product that I'm making, how will it be used and intended purpose from a regulatory perspective, and what problem exactly is it solving in terms of value proposition' and that it needs to be 'really clearly defined early days and done so in a way that's cognizant of the perspectives of the users, patients, the public and commissioners'. She explains that developers often have multiple plausible but unproven value claims, and that the best thing they could is to focus on demonstrating one or two claims really well. The value claim should inform evidence generation, such as 'how long your study needs to run, how many sites should be involved, and how many participants, what outcome data and comparators to collect, and diversity of participants and sites'. It also 'has implications for the business model and the market access strategy'.

Once you have identified and defined the problem that you are trying to solve, the next steps are as follows:

First, identify potential solutions that could work. Start simple and try to find a solution that does not involve AI. Only consider the next step, if no solution can be found without adding AI. Otherwise go to step three.

Second, consider the possibilities if the solution includes AI. Does that now solve the problem? Don't be tempted to add 'as much AI as possible'; keep it as light touch as possible. Another important point to consider is when AI should be incorporated. It may be that the

AI functionality is best placed later in the product roadmap, once an MVP or non-AI based solution is launched to solve a proportion of the problem, and gains traction and a user base.

Finally, do a sense check to ensure we are solving the problem and it's the same problem we set out to solve.

The roadmap

The roadmap below sets out a five stage process, starting from identifying the problem through to monitoring and improving the AI solution following launch.

The five stages of the roadmap are:

1. **Identify** - builds on the pre-roadmap activity of asking the question 'What problem are you trying to solve?' to develop the problem statement and the concept of what the solution needs to be able to do further, and to validate this with key stakeholders

2. **Design** - work with key stakeholders to design a solution that takes into account clinical and operational workflows, and start identifying business case levers and regulatory requirements

3. **Develop** - integrate validation and regulation requirements to develop and refine a solution that is scalable and meets 'enterprise' standards

4. **Implement** - support the gradual roll out and related change management activities to validate the solution and gather evidence of benefits

5. **Monitor and improve** - support the realisation of planned benefits while working to continually improve the solution and continuing to operate in a manner compliant with regulations

Taking a structured and gradual approach is crucial as is the various stakeholder groups working collaboratively to achieve the common objective.

The stakeholder groups considered are as follows:

- **Innovators** - designers and developers of solutions, including start-ups, technology companies, healthcare organisations
- **Health operators and systems** - individual providers of health and care services (for example, hospitals or primary care providers), or collections of providers (likely regions or healthcare 'systems')
- **Funders** - payers (including insurance companies), and providers of capital, including public sector, grant funders, as well as private investors
- **End users** - those who will use and benefits from the product, including healthcare professionals, wider healthcare workforce, public, patients, family and carers
- **Compliance** - individuals and organisations involved in the developing, implementation, monitoring and enforcing of legal and regulatory standards (including data privacy and information governance)

The roadmap below takes a grid approach to lay out each stage for each of the stakeholder groups as they take the journey from 'Identity' through to 'Monitor and improve'.

To ensure mutual success, it also highlights the 'commitment' each group needs to make in undertaking the 'journey'.

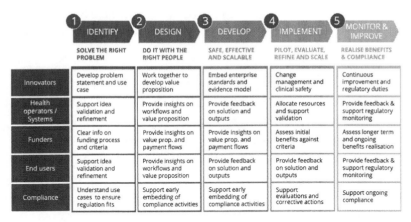

	1 IDENTIFY	2 DESIGN	3 DEVELOP	4 IMPLEMENT	5 MONITOR & IMPROVE
	SOLVE THE RIGHT PROBLEM	DO IT WITH THE RIGHT PEOPLE	SAFE, EFFECTIVE AND SCALABLE	PILOT, EVALUATE, REFINE AND SCALE	REALISE BENEFITS & COMPLIANCE
Innovators	Develop problem statement and use case	Work together to develop value proposition	Embed enterprise standards and evidence model	Change management and clinical safety	Continuous improvement and regulatory duties
Health operators / Systems	Support idea validation and refinement	Provide insights on workflows and value proposition	Provide feedback on solution and outputs	Allocate resources and support validation	Provide feedback & support regulatory monitoring
Funders	Clear info on funding process and criteria	Provide insights on value prop. and payment flows	Provide insights on value prop. and payment flows	Assess initial benefits against criteria	Assess longer term and ongoing benefits realisation
End users	Support idea validation and refinement	Provide insights on workflows and value proposition	Provide feedback on solution and outputs	Provide feedback on solution and outputs	Provide feedback & support regulatory monitoring
Compliance	Understand use cases to ensure regulation fits	Support early embedding of compliance activities	Support early embedding of compliance activities	Support evaluations and corrective actions	Support ongoing compliance

Figure 10: Roadmap to more successful adoption and scaling of AI in healthcare

The Innovator's journey

In the 'Identify' stage, it is so important to clearly define the actual existing problem, so that you successfully solve the right problem later on.

Breght Boschker was the CTO of SkinVision from 2016 until 2021, and remains involved as a senior advisor. SkinVision is an AI based solution that helps users self-examine skin lesions and get advice using their mobile phones[10]. Breght enjoys building products and helping non-technical companies with technology strategy and technical companies with product strategy. He joined SkinVision after helping them through an investment round.

The company has gone through technology and clinical validation phases and are in the process of business model validation and refinement. Breght describes the challenge they have as a dual sales problem. First, is raising awareness, making people aware that one in five people globally get skin cancer and that more than 50% of cancers occur in the skin. Second, is to convince users that SkinVision has a solution that can help. He says that the second challenge proved difficult in a general population. Breght relates that a lot of people don't want to think about cancer; they are only seeking peace of mind. If they pay to use the app (a 'spot check') and the assessment says they are fine, they typically stop using the app.

The team have been thinking a lot over the past two years about patient journeys and how to move away from a 'spot check' approach to a more complete service offering. Breght explains that to make the transition they needed to start from the user point of view and their journey and ask, 'What would users want to see?' He identifies the need to move to a more broad approach, where if users have any question about skin – whether it's a simple pimple or cancer – they can use this. The SkinVision technology can't answer all of these questions, and a team of human dermatologists complement the algorithms (linking back to the point earlier in this book on complementing humans). For the questions that the algorithm can safely answer, it's about having the right controls in place and ultimately integrating both technology and human expertise to help the user at the appropriate point in their journey, he explains. It would then move the company towards a population health management approach where users will use the solution on an ongoing basis, prompted by proactive triggers at appropriate times. Because skin changes over time, Breght compares checking one's skin to going to the dentist twice a year.

Key points to consider when defining the problem and identifying a solution are shared below in a handy 'cheat sheet'.

CHEAT SHEET

Define a problem and identify a solution

- **What is the problem?** There needs to be a clear definition of the problem. You need to be able to explain it objectively (and quantify it) and in context of the operating environment of healthcare. The explanation needs to be validated with stakeholders from within the industry

- **Is it worth solving?** Once the validated problem statement has been developed, you need to understand the potential benefits of a solution. Is the problem important enough to invest time and resources solving (not all problems are)? An additional point to consider here is the cost of change to implement the change and whether the benefits of solving the problem justifies it

- **Co-design with healthcare.** Do not design and develop solutions in isolation. Involving clinicians and other healthcare workforce, and patients will provide valuable insights to how to maximise the benefits of the solution and will help you avoid common pitfalls. It will also help develop champions of your solution, greatly helping with early adoption and credibility

- **Is it only a technology solution?** Do not focus only on the technology. The most advanced model, trained on the perfect data will not have any impact if it can't integrate with healthcare systems and processes in a way that adds value and does not create a lot of additional work for clinicians

- **Is healthcare ready?** Is the organisation ready? Sometimes, it will not be you (or your solution) but 'them'. The overall maturity of the healthcare system and competing priorities for its limited resources may mean that it's not the right time (yet). On a similar vein, an under resourced hospital with a stretched workforce that does have the necessary skills and experience will not provide an enabling environment

When you move on to the 'Design' stage, developing a solution by yourself is very risky. Translation from 'in silico' to healthcare is not a straight path. Working together with end users and other key stakeholders, whether you are developing commercially or conducting research, is really important. More examples were discussed within the AI is not an 'island' sub-section in Chapter Six.

Key points to consider when developing a value proposition are illustrated in another 'cheat sheet' below.

CHEAT SHEET

Develop a value proposition

- **What is the solution?** It all goes back to the problem you are trying to solve. This is always the best place to start. To again ensure that there is a clear problem you are solving and that it is one worth solving. From the problem, you can move on to describing the proposed solution

- **What are the benefits?** Potential benefits need to be clearly defined and quantified (either from a patient outcome, financial, efficiency or other perspective). In doing so, it is very important to define and quantify the baseline - for example, currently it takes one hour to complete this activity or the accuracy of diagnosing this disease is 50%. You must also consider how benefits can be evaluated and measured after deployment of the solution to increase the likelihood of full benefits realisation and course correction if things go off track

- **Does it take into account full life costs?** When articulating costs, you must take a holistic view. First, from a buyer perspective, for a successful implementation of the solution the costs will not only be the direct costs associated with the solution (for example, licensing costs) and will include investment in process and organisational changes required, as well as project and change management support. Second, you and the buyer must consider and articulate relevant costs following the deployment - for example, for maintenance and updates to the solution, hosting and other infrastructure costs, and ongoing compliance requirements and related costs

- **What are the key success factors?** While each situation and solution may put greater importance on different factors, there are common factors across all scenarios. For example, have you engaged and co-designed the solution with end users and other relevant stakeholder groups? Do you have the required levels of evidence to support the claimed benefits? Does the solution comply with all the required regulations? Can it integrate into clinical pathways and related processes in a manner acceptable to clinicians?

- **Who pays? How do they buy and pay for it?** Due to the complex nature of healthcare and the fact that the patient often 'travels' along a pathway across various care settings and organisations it is often not clear who should pay (for example, if the solution prevents patients being admitted into a hospital and if the hospital gets paid based on the number patients it treats, why will the hospital be incentivised to pay?). If there is someone willing to pay, how do they buy? In Europe and in the public sector, there are regulations and legal requirements related to competitive tendering and transparency. How exactly will the supplier get paid - for example, does there need to be a 'reimbursement code', which will allow the claiming of a certain cost based on the solution and the circumstances of its use

It is very important that you get an early understanding of the regulatory requirements for your ideas. Sources such as the MHRA Innovation Office can provide free and accurate information and signpost you to further sources.

As David Higgins highlights in his second paper[3], it is important to be clear about the 'intended use' (the suppliers declaration of what the valid use cases are) as it impacts how the models are built, evaluated and how clinical trials are designed. In order to get to a clear intended use, we need to understand the correct solution as early as possible.

The intended use also determines whether a solution is classed as a medical device and therefore the need to conform with regulations such as the EU Medical Device Regulations or the UK Medical Device Regulations 2002. This would also then require compliance to standards such as ISO 13485 (quality management systems), ISO 14971 (risk management) and ISO 62304 (software life cycle processes). There are also wider standards being developed, for example the British Standards Institute (BSI) is developing an AI standard for suppliers and health organisations which is due to be published by the end of 2023[11].

Neville Young advises that innovators need to be realistic about the benefits they are describing. He further explains the difference between making a 'saving' for the NHS (genuine cost reductions) and making the same amount of efficiency or productivity gains (which will not always result in a cost saving). Being clear about the benefits you are describing and the supporting evidence for these claims is vital.

When it comes to outcomes and evidence generation, Clíodhna Ní Ghuidhir has the following advice. 'Be really clear in your study of how any kind of cost claims or cost reduction claims that you are putting forward have been thought through'. She adds that 'it needs to be the most granular thinking and you need the most detail-oriented people who are really willing to go through the pain of thinking through what exactly is the intervention, how is it going to be used and by whom, and therefore will it lead to a meaningful time efficiency?' Like Neville, she asks, 'Does that time efficiency then convert into actual saved money?'

On the front line of healthcare delivery, the systems and processes that support it must be robust. Within the 'Develop' phase, you must build a solution that aligns with industry best practice, and is scalable and secure. A good example of this was discussed in the Sepsis Watch case study in Chapter Three related to integrating appropriately with the EHR system, considering security aspects and providing a support function for the solution.

Ask, how can the accuracy of the solution be proven? Secondly, how can you measure the cost-effectiveness of the solution?

Ensuring clinical safety is a key aspect in gaining the trust of clinicians and in deploying a solution that does not cause harm to patients. Emma Selby says that she faced a lot of pushback during the early days at Wysa on clinical risk, particularly when she would go to interviews for grants. People were nervous about the idea of any level of automation or autonomy in mental health, especially in the context of users who were planning to self-harm or commit suicide. The concerns were around how Wysa would stop that from happening. Wysa recognises if you are using language that indicates intention to harm yourself or others, and signposts users to the most appropriate helpline when they can get support. Emma explains that her approach was to strip it back to basics, explaining that when these users phone the office at midnight saying they are feeling suicidal, they get a voicemail message. The Wysa solution is at least equivalent to this, and overall it would be improving the patient outcomes across a number of other areas.

Emma confirms that they did a lot of work around clinical risk management and compliance to DCB-0129: Clinical Risk Management: its Application in the Manufacture of Health IT Systems[12]. (This is a standard defined by NHS Digital for suppliers developing clinical IT solutions for use in the NHS to enable identification of hazards, mitigation of risks to a level as low as reasonably practicable, and ongoing monitoring following implementation to ensure the solution remains safe for clinical use). She explains that she took a step back from sales and focused on getting clinical risk management right, and demonstrated that Wysa can detect the relevant words and flag up appropriate support services. This investment and focus has led to one of the highest clinical risk ratings on the ORCHA platform[13] (which reviews and certifies digital health solutions), and being able to confidently stand in front of people to explain that the solution can actually reduce the risk for these users.

The 'Implement' stage must be planned and managed in a structured way to take into account key elements.

Another 'cheat sheet'! For developing the implementation plan, below.

CHEAT SHEET

Develop an implementation plan

- **What is the journey?** You need to develop a staged plan, supporting the gradual implementation and building of momentum. The first stage should revolve around a pilot, to provide a manageable environment and scope. It is important to consider quick wins to build momentum and help gain key stakeholder buy-in

- **Have you looked under the hood?** A clever AI solution will not fix messy workflows. Successful AI solutions have structured and thoughtful workflows that support and enhance the potential of technology. If workflows are messy, you need to fix them first

---

- **Will you have the support?** This is two fold. First, from a stakeholder perspective, you need buy-in from both the front line workforce, and operations and management who will authorise funding. You must identify champions who will fight for you and invest in change management before and during implementation. Second, is from a technical perspective. This covers both the environment the solution will deploy into (for example, architecture and integration with other systems) and the quality and future 'supply' of data you will need

- **Are you compliant and will you have the evidence?** There are some elements of compliance that you will need before you start including information governance and clinical safety sign offs. Depending on the scope of implementation and levels of control, hence the importance of pilots, it may be feasible to gradually provide compliance for certain elements. It is also important to engage early with information governance, clinical safety and wider AI (or medical device) regulatory bodies to ensure the required processes are baked into your plan. Developing a clear plan that considers and gathers efficacy and outcomes data from as early as possible (and structures the implementation accordingly) will be valuable in demonstrating both the accuracy and cost-effectiveness of your solution

- **What happens after a successful deployment?** As Sundeep Khanna points out, of the key elements to consider is the impact on the operating model, for example what are the changes needed to current roles and how do you deal with the time the solution frees up? Successful implementation plans also consider and provide resources for the post-deployment phase to cover important elements such as maintenance, continuous improvement of the solution and surveillance to ensure the ongoing safety of the solution

Dr Matt Stammers suggests that the 'proof comes in the pudding'; when people see results, they change their minds. The hospital is in the process of a stage two pilot project called 'Scale, spread and embed', led by Imperial College London and Imperial College Healthcare NHS Trust. The initiative takes the free text information from the NHS friends and family test and provides insights in real time that can be used to plan clinical and operational activity. The solution has been developed and validated at multiple sites, but some key stakeholders don't quite see the benefit yet. Matt says, 'when they do, there will be no turning back'.

Yosef Safi Harb reflects on his experience developing the Happitech product, and a lesson learnt around the design of clinical study. He says that their clinical study took three years, which was a relatively long time for digital health. A key lesson was learning how to optimise for busy clinical workflows. He explains that, unlike large medical device companies or pharmaceutical companies with significant resources to invest in dedicated clinical research resources, start-ups need to account for the realities of the clinical front line. For example, Yosef says they did a cardioversion (a procedure to restore the normal rhythm of the heart) study, where a patient comes in, gets a cardioversion and the nurse needs to be there before and after to take a measurement. If the clinical nurse, who is supporting many clinical studies as well as her clinical role, gets called away and they miss getting the reading in time before the patient goes home, they just lose the patient from the study. Therefore, a simple and 'easy' workflow is required when designing clinical studies to consider the resource constraints and to capture as much information as possible with minimal impact on clinician time.

Following a successful implementation, your work does not end. In the 'Monitor and improve' stage, and from a regulatory perspective, you will have an obligation to review continuing efficacy and identify any potential issues. From a continuous improvement perspective, you need to monitor for changes in clinical practice and underlying data to ensure efficacy and opportunities for improvement.

The health operator or systems' journey

In the 'Identify' and 'Design' stages, one of your key roles is working with Innovators and End users to support them on the focus areas.

In the 'Identify' stage, you need to work with Innovators and End users to support the development of the problem statement, to validate it and help refine it as per the 'Define a problem and identify a solution' cheat sheet above.

In the 'Design' stage, you need to work with Innovators and End users to support the development of the solution and the value proposition as per the 'Develop a value proposition' cheat sheet above.

Limited 'working together' in these early stages can be driven by various stakeholder groups For example, a 2020 survey by McKinsey involving interviews and online surveys of AI and digital health leaders, healthcare professionals, inventors and start-up founders revealed interesting results[14]. Only 14% of start-ups leaders thought that it was important to get healthcare professional input in the early phases. Healthcare professionals didn't see value in the private sector's input in aggregating and analysing data, or in helping upskill staff. You could play a role in educating both sides and bringing both parties to the table to work together during these crucial phases and activities to ensure a solution that addresses real problems and delivers meaningful outcomes is developed.

David Higgins says that the biggest benefit his clients cite when using his framework is that it pulls multidisciplinary teams onto the same page. He says, 'in my experience, treating the domains separately leads to the domain experts maintaining their blind spots, and everybody else ignoring domains which are not their own'. David suggests that even having a single kick-off where multi-disciplinary teams work on a common approach can 'lead to massive light-bulb moments, for example where ML engineers finally understand what is important to clinicians'.

During the 'Develop' stage, you should provide feedback on both the solution and the planned outcomes. You must be realistic in terms of the effort it takes to support innovators develop products and also what problem they are attempting to solve, and do it incrementally as part of a roadmap.

Paolo Melissa is a senior radiographer at the George Eliot Hospital NHS Trust in England. The hospital worked with a supplier as part of the NHS AI Lab's Skunkworks programme. The problems they were looking to solve is to support the alignment of CT scans during comparisons in oncology reporting and to support the identification of lesions in the scans.

Paolo explains that when comparing two scans to see any changes in the size of a lesion, to identify new lesions or assess the reduction in the size of the lesion due to treatment, the two scans have to be manually aligned. This is a laborious and time consuming process, and you can only do it on one axis at a time. Some lesions are prone to be missed; some studies showing that up to 30% lesions can be missed.

The initial stage of the project was a 12 week proof of concept. While there were two main problems to solve, Paolo explained that they decided to focus on the alignment one as the first step. One of the next considerations was the amount of training data they could provide. Initially it was planned to provide 'thousands' of scans. However, Paolo soon realised the challenge when reviewing the time it took to prepare one scan: while some of the process could be automated, he still had to select certain 'windows' of the scan that was of interest, and use another tool to complete the anonymisation of the scans to remove patient identifiable details before sharing with the supplier. In the end a more realistic 100 scans was agreed. The proof of concept achieved very good results in achieving automated alignment. This illustrates an important point regarding realistic scope (how many and which part of the problem to try and solve) and planning for and resourcing activities such as data preparation and provision, when considering how to develop and implement AI solutions. Ultimately, Paulo concludes, 'if the data requirement would have stayed in the thousands of scans, this could have probably led to the failure of the project'.

In the 'Implement' phases you must identify and invest in making the right resources available to support the implementation and validation. Careful consideration and investment needs to be made to ensure support commitments, and the demands on healthcare professionals, are sustainable. From a validation perspective, the scarcity of data analyst and general AI skills may be a challenge, therefore an assessment of internal capability and capacity should be completed and where necessary, the resources can be sourced from outside the organisation.

Post implementation, you need to provide ongoing feedback to support continuous improvement of the solution and support regulatory monitoring (including access to and sharing within proper controls and regulations).

What do funder's need to do?

There are two main groups of funders; governments and large institutions largely fund infrastructure and private investors largely fund products.

In the 'Identify' stage, the focus should be on providing clear information on the funding sources and criteria to obtain it. On infrastructure funding, from a public funder (for example, governments funding health systems and operators) and grant funder perspective, this will be sharing information on the 'pots' of funding that is available for innovators, and what the priorities are (for example, certain specialities or specific challenges). From a private investor point of view, it will be about information on early (seed) funding available and what you are looking for in solutions and in the founding team.

During the 'Design' and 'Develop' phases, both groups of funders should build on the previous stage to support the Innovators develop a robust value proposition. Infrastructure funders should help them consider and align with appropriate payment mechanisms (for example, reimbursement for activities or outcomes delivered). The thinking on reimbursements for AI solutions are in early stages and there is much more work that needs to be done at national level to develop it.

During the remaining two stages, the focus should be on working with Innovators, and Health operators and systems to assess benefits against the stated value proposition and ensure the maximum benefits are realised for patients, the workforce and system as a whole. From a private investor perspective, benefits realisation is equally important to enable scaling, and ultimately the increase the value of the solution, and therefore the company.

The end users' journey

The focus during the first two stages are similar to that of a Health operator and system, and you should work closely together.

In the 'Identify' stage, you need to work with Innovators and End users to support the development of the problem statement, to validate it and help refine it as per the 'Define a problem and identify a solution' cheat sheet above.

In the 'Design' stage, you need to work with Innovators and End users to support the development of the solution and the value proposition as per the 'Develop a value proposition' cheat sheet above.

During 'Develop' and 'Implement', you will need to work closely with the Innovator in getting the solution (and the operator or system ready) by providing feedback on the solution. Once deployed, you will need to help identify and assess the outputs against the intended results.

In the longer term, you should be involved in supporting continuous improvement by making suggestions for refinements and additional features, and advise the Innovators on changes in clinical practice.

You would also support ongoing monitoring of results and providing feedback to ensure the solution is compliant with regulations, and is safe for patients.

Making compliance work

If you are a regulator or are responsible for ensuring information governance standards are met, how can you help?

During the 'Identify' phase, you should work with Innovators, and Health operators and systems to understand the ideas and solutions being considered to support discussions on how regulation and compliance applies.

Providing guidance at this stage is useful. One example is the Data Ethics Canvas, developed by the Open Data Institute[15]. The Canvas is designed to help those who collect, use and share data to identify and manage ethical issues. It elucidates questions and considerations in key areas including data sources, impact on people, and communication. Another good example is the *Explaining decisions made with AI guidance* developed by the Information Commissioner's Office and the Alan Turing Institute in the UK[16]. It provides advice on how to explain the processes, services and decisions related to your AI solutions. First, aimed at Data Protection Officers and compliance teams, it defines the key concepts including AI itself, legal frameworks and risks and benefits. Second, aimed at technical teams, it covers practicalities including how to tailor explanations based on industry and use case, how to select explainable models and how to make the best of less explainable models. Third, aimed at senior management, covers what needs to be done at an organisational level including policy, documentation, and roles to enable provision of explanations to the relevant individuals.

The earlier activities are planned and started, the earlier they are embedded within the solution, the greater likelihood of a safe implementation, trust in the solution deployed, and sustainable operation and scaling.

Johan Ordish and Russell Pearson highlight three key success factors for organisations who successfully navigate the regulatory landscape. First, is to think about regulation early. They explain that this allows embedding of integral elements, such as Quality Management Systems, crucial to developing safe systems and to demonstrating compliance with regulation later on. Second, is the culture of the company: understanding how to make a compliant device, how to engage with regulators, understanding patient needs and having a network of brands and products rather than a single product. Third, is multidisciplinary teams with skills in user centric design, medical devices, data science, and clinical awareness.

During 'Design' and 'Develop' phases, you should also support Innovators, Health operators and systems, and End users by answering questions and providing support as they develop their compliance activities.

During the 'Implement' phase, support should be provided (working with Health operators and systems, and End users) to review outputs and processes to ensure the solutions are compliant. It would not be appropriate for you to do this directly. Developing and partnering with a network of individuals and organisations that will have the necessary knowledge and practical experience of developing solutions will be a good alternative. These individuals and organisations can work closely with innovators to help them refine processes and take any corrective action needed to ensure compliant solutions that are safe for its intended use.

During the 'Monitor and improve' stage, you should support the dissemination of the information needed so that Innovators, Health operators and systems, and End users understand their roles and responsibilities in ensuring the continual safety and efficacy of the solution. This includes ensuring that the appropriate governance processes and agreements are in place to cover the continual sharing of data.

The enablers

Our attention has been on the 'doing' and the 'present moment' during the various stages of the solution lifecycle.

Related to the five stages on the roadmap, there are a number of enablers that increase the likelihood of success of implementation and adoption of AI solutions. These are a combination of elements that need to be 'done' during the solution lifecycle and that need to be 'there' during the solution lifecycle.

The enablers can be considered across five key areas as follows:

- **Data** - access to high quality, varied, representative, and collated data
- **Risk management and building of trust** - compliance with regulation and other elements of the solution that promote trust
- **Collaboration** - working together as individuals and organisations to share insights and achieve better outcomes collectively
- **Complement humans** - supporting successful evaluation, selection and implementation of solutions to maximise benefits realisation
- **Sustainability** - investment and availability of resources to enable successfully implement and maintain solutions

The key enablers across each of the areas are highlighted in the diagram below.

Data	Good quality, varied data pipelines	Linkage & harmonisation	Data ownership & sharing
Risk management & building trust	Compliant with regulation and good practice	Minimisation of bias	Transparency & explainability
Collaboration	Sharing outputs and lessons learnt	Ecosystem enablers inc. APIs & open standards	Commercial - frameworks and modular requirements
Complement humans	Change management & stakeholder buy-in	Digital skills & how to evaluate AI solutions	Consider workflows & resource implications
Sustainability	Infrastructure needed to support data flows	Capability to validate models & implement solutions	Resources to monitor compliance & maintain solutions

Figure 11: Key enablers to more successful adoption and scaling of AI in healthcare

Data

Access to data is paramount. The quality of training data available is central: sufficient volume, quality, and representative of the population of interest. The second element is that there needs to be a regular 'flow' of this data, and it not only be available as a 'one off'.

Yosef explains how he used an innovative crowdsourcing campaign to gather training data for Happitech. The campaign, called 'Heart for Heart', was in partnership with the Dutch Heart Foundation. People could contribute their data using an iPhone app. The contribution included 90 seconds of their heart rhythm and data on risk factors. He explained that the contributors could decide which data they wanted to share, and that once shared it was anonymised before being shared with researchers. Informed consent was recorded using Apple ResearchKit. The initiative gathered over 15,000 datasets from more than 70 countries[17]. It was really important to Happitech, Yosef says, to develop algorithms based on real world data in addition to the slow data gathering process though hospitals.

Data collected from various sources and systems must be linked so that patient journeys across time and care settings can be analysed.

'To enable AI to do a better job and if we're really going to leverage the potential of AI, we are going to have to work much harder on enabling sharing data, integrating data and linking data', Maneesh Juneja says. He points out that EHRs only have a 'snapshot' and there is 'all this other information about my health outside of the hospital that is not easily available or even when it is, nobody wants to link it together'. Maneesh believes that 'if we want a 360-degree view of someone's life and what influences their health in the real world, we need to start having honest conversations about linking data together'. 'Let's do it in a trusted way', he says, 'and let's be ambitious about that, because otherwise we're not going to deliver on the promise of AI revolutionising healthcare'.

Data harmonisation is required to effectively collate different datasets to account for differing practices in how the same variables are recorded by different organisations and regions. The open standards and common data models discussed earlier will help.

The ownership of data is also crucial. GDPR provides users with rights to data held by organisations. Barry Moult reiterates that 'an organisation must know what data it processes' and that in the UK, this must fall in line with the Article 30 of the UK GDPR. He also highlights the 7 UK GDPR principles which need to be applied; lawfulness, fairness and transparency, purpose limitation, data minimisation, accuracy, storage limitation, Integrity and confidentiality (security) and accountability. Finally, he says that organisations should 'clearly understand the type of data (for example, personal and special category data) and actors (data controllers versus data processors) to help correctly decide what data is processed and why'.

With EHR and other systems, existing commercial arrangements may mean that ownership of data is unclear or that getting access to the data held by suppliers is prohibitively expensive. Barry highlights that 'ownership of data can be very subjective'.

He explains what needs to be clearly defined in the contract: who exactly is the data controller, data processor (and joint controller), what data is shared and who else can access the data. He advocates that a DPIA is completed to document and assess any risks or potential risks. Barry also suggests a 'sharing agreement', although not legally binding, could give further clarity on what and how data is being shared.

Being able to easily share data is necessary. Tesco Clubcard has processes and underlying technology to support transfer of a customer's data to third parties easily[18]. Non-fungible tokens (NFTs) are blockchain based unique identifiers that are linked to an asset. (The artist known as Beeple sold an NFT for $69m in 2021!) It has been suggested that, notwithstanding technical challenges that still need to be worked through, NFTs present an interesting way for patients to control access to (and the terms by which access is granted) their de-identified medical data[19].

Risk management and building trust

Compliance with regulations and with clinical safety elements discussed previously will provide the required base level of confidence to health systems, end users and funders.

When minimising bias, both the composition of the data to ensure appropriate representation and the methodology (for example, as previously described incorrectly using cost as a proxy for complexity of care), must be considered. David Higgins, in his paper on regulation[3], highlights a common mistake that occurs. He says that projects usually start off at world class centres of excellence and the cohort of patients there is quite different to the wider providers (for example, higher risk at the world class centres). Therefore, further training data and evaluation is needed before it can be safely deployed.

Breght Boschker highlights the importance of metadata (references and information about the characteristics of the data) in understanding the origins and distribution of the data (for example, which countries, which demographics, which devices were used to collect the data and for which individual). This additional information helps curate a training dataset that is truly representative of the population of interest.

Transparency and explainability of how the model works and derives the outputs is useful in developing trust with healthcare professionals (and meeting regulatory requirements). It is also useful for healthcare professionals in explaining treatment plans to their patients. However, explainability can be a complex concept because human interpretation of the outputs of AI models will be based on assumptions and may be influenced by an individual's way of thinking. Therefore, explainability needs to include a clear and complete description of the output and rationale. This needs to be complemented by training for end users to enable interpretation in a consistent and 'as intended' manner. Having said that, the drive for explainability needs to be balanced with compromises in accuracy and the general background that in the practice of medicine, certain areas such as sepsis (as described within the Sepsis Watch case study) cannot be well explained at the moment.

Collaboration

As evidenced by the poor performance of models developed during Covid-19, working together and sharing information is key. Sharing results and lessons learned helps make the most of investments, enables faster going to market and reduces mistakes.

Arfah Farooq highlights that, for her, the best way communities can add value is talking about their work in the open. For example, with NHS AI Lab's Skunkworks, the code is published openly on GitHub (an online repository where source code can be version controlled, shared, and collaborated on in a structured manner), enabling other hospitals to review the work and adopt the approach and code.

Dr Basab Bhattacharya confirms that vendors approach managers at individual hospitals with solutions to what they think the problems are, rather than the actual problems. He highlights the importance of clinicians working together across organisations to discuss and develop areas of clinical need and where AI could help.

To enable efficient access to data (to maximise value from collected data to the healthcare system) and for solutions (such as AI, where the current outputs are best there is a narrow focus) to provide a holistic solution aimed at a large and complex problem, there are two key enablers. First are APIs (and wherever possible separation of the application and data layer) to make access to data within the system and the flow between them easier. Second are open technology standards that support standardised flows of data across different solutions.

The above needs to be complemented from a commercial perspective. First, there must be established and widely available routes for purchasing the solutions, with associated payment models and funding allocated. Furthermore, to promote true collaboration the commercial constructs must allow for requirements to be modular and reflect the specific 'niches' so that different solutions (AI and non-AI) can come together effectively.

Complement humans

AI can help best by working alongside people to enhance productivity and allow them to focus their time on activities that maximise their skills and experience.

Enablers in this area fall into two categories. First are those that support the successful implementation of solutions and realisation of potential benefits.

Consider and invest in the change management activities needed to support implementation and gain the buy-in required. This is directly related to the 'Will you have the support' point highlighted in the implementation plan cheat sheet. The second element is to understand existing workflows so that the solution fully integrates with it (rather than duplicate processes or cause additional work for the healthcare professionals) and to identify and account for impact on the healthcare workforce (for example, time they need to allocate to the project).

The second category relates to upskilling the workforce and ensuring that they have the capabilities required to evaluate (understand what is available in the market and develop a base understanding of benefits and risks) and operate (for example, clinicians understanding how to interpret accuracy metrics and appreciating the limitations of AI).

Sustainability

Sustainability is focused on the longevity of the solution and the benefits it can deliver.

Technology related enablers include the infrastructure required to support data flows and access. These are secure environments that can collate, store and process data, as well as infrastructure that can facilitate secure flow of structured data external to the organisation in a repeatable manner.

Secondly are those capability and human resource related. For example, the health systems need to have individuals with the skills and experience to support model validation and implementation of solutions during the 'Develop' and 'Implement' stages. Following this, resources are needed that support the healthcare organisations and systems conduct the required maintenance and refinement (working with the Innovators) and to support the required data flows and validation required for ongoing surveillance and efficacy monitoring.

Depending on the solution, the context and setting of implementation, certain enablers will be more important. For example, transparency and explainability for results will be less important for an AI solution automating and enhancing back office functions, compared to supporting the delivery of front line clinical services.

The above enablers can be applicable at three levels, solution or project, organisational, and regional or national. For example, minimisation of bias is mainly applicable at a solution or project level. Workflow or resource considerations can be applicable at both organisational, and regional or national level. Sharing and linkage of data is applicable at regional or national level.

CHAPTER 9

LET'S DO THIS

The potential of AI in healthcare is an area I am both optimistic and passionate about. I hope we can make it work as the potential benefits to patient outcomes, healthcare professionals and the overall ecosystem will be enormous.

For everyone reading this book, these are my key takeaways.

1. **Take a moment to pause** from working on any solutions. Consider the problem you are trying to solve and where in the roadmap you are, to identify the key things you need to focus on.
2. Bear in mind that success will not be achieved by individual stakeholders acting alone. We need to **work together.**

Clíodhna Ní Ghuidhir believes that for AI to really work, there needs to a deep partnership approach between adopters and innovators, and 'mutual understanding and agreements about how data is then going to be collected and how that data will then be used for improving the product and ensuring that things don't go wrong or that if things go wrong (e.g. if performance drifts), action is taken at the right time'. She also points out that 'it requires bravery because you might get things wrong and also bravery in terms of being willing to take on the accountability for getting it right'.

FOUR KEY CONSIDERATIONS FOR FUNDERS AND POLICY MAKERS

Dr Sukhmeet Panesar is the deputy director for strategy and development directorate of the Chief Data and Analytics Officer at NHSE&I. Whilst working as a junior doctor, he took the opportunity to work for a year with the Chief Medical Officer, which led to further opportunities with the National Patient Safety Agency (NPSA) and the WHO. He then decided to leave clinical practice to focus on management consulting before moving back to the NHS as the strategy lead for the Data, Analysis and Intelligence Service (DAIS). He describes his current role as 'thinking about how we bring lots of disparate analytical teams together to create an enterprise, Amazon-style outfit that uses the latest technologies, empowers its workforce, and delivers real decision-making insights'. Sukhmeet explains that his current areas of focus are first on population health and data analytics at scale (for example, using the correct platforms and changing people's mindsets), second on training, development, and professionalising the role of the analyst, and third on collaboration.

Sukhmeet believes that organisations such as NHSE&I, which began life as a commissioning organisation, need to move away from 'purely being a buyer' to more of an enabler. At a high level, this means providing money, expertise and providing support for 'people who want to start innovating and doing things'.

A favourable environment for change can't be created overnight or by one of the above stakeholder groups 'trying harder' but investing in selected enablers will make a significant impact. This will require careful thinking and planning at national level (as decisions will have knock on effects on other elements of healthcare delivery), and require significant investment and buy-in from various stakeholders who will need to support implementation of the changes.

The most important of these enablers and key elements are the following four.

The importance of curated training data

Providing wider access, with appropriate controls depending on the dataset, to curated training data sets will be transformative.

The NHS, Sukhmeet says, is a 'very closed system when it comes to letting third parties, innovators or entrepreneurs play with the data'.

It has got better but so much more needs to be done. He says that they will often 'have wonderful conversations with advanced analytic firms and AI firms, discuss great ideas' and unfortunately, we don't have a mechanism for them to access the data. Sometimes they would spend up to 16 weeks going back and forth before having to say, 'You can't have the data, why don't you use a public data set instead?' He believes that there is a huge opportunity in getting 'the industry to play in a safe, ethical, meaningful manner with our data'. 'And working collaboratively, it's not really them versus us'.

Dr Jonny Pearson highlights that when you look at the boom in AI more widely, it has always been when there has been large, well curated datasets available to the public. These large datasets, including databases of text and images, make for excellent training datasets allowing innovators to develop and test new algorithms. Jonny believes these types of datasets, either synthetically generated or collated real data with appropriate consent or anonymisation, will be needed in the next five years to drive innovation. This innovation will come through exploration of the data, he says, comparisons within and identification of opportunities that follow the insights gained.

He explained that these datasets will help overcome a common problem he sees, which is that if someone approaches a healthcare organisation with an idea for a model, it takes months to setup a data sharing agreement and eventually when the work is done and a lot of effort is spent, the data quality is found to be inadequate or the model doesn't quite work. If we can allow a model to be developed and tested on public datasets, which provide higher levels of confidence on its viability, it will be a much more efficient and cost-effective process, and one that will be more attractive for innovators to pursue.

Professor David Lowe agrees. 'If you are a small start-up, training data is hard to get hold of and it's a vicious circle... the lack of training data leads to more models being biased and not generalisable'. The opportunity is around making selected datasets (for example, a heart failure dataset with case controls and demographic data from Glasgow) available to a wider audience with the appropriate governance and access controls in place, and through 'safe haven' type platforms. Similar to Jonathan, David believes that this will allow healthcare to generate interest and engagement, and to 'show us what you can do with this data' and to then 'tell us what data you need' to develop it further.

Harshana Liyanage explains that government organisations are owners of a large number of important data sources that could be leveraged for developing and validating machine learning applications at scale. He says that it is then possible to incorporate a range of data sources by conducting the experimental work and develop innovative solutions. There have also been recent technical developments that are helpful.

Andrew Ng elaborates on data-centric AI and with it, the shift in focus recently from refining algorithms to refining the data[1]. With all the work done over the last decade on improving the code, it is now more productive to leave the neural network architecture alone and focus on ways of improving the data, Andrew affirms. A small amount (for example, 50 good examples) can help develop something useful – a shift from 'big data' to 'good data'. This has two steps. First, pre-trained models and fine tuning them using a small amount of data. Second, identifying specific areas of poor quality (for example, 30 images out of a dataset of 10,000 that are labelled inconsistently) so those can be relabelled (which could also help with bias, where adjusting the subset of data on which the bias is based is much more efficient than trying to adjust the overall model).

Transfer learning, that is, training on a large dataset and then retraining the model on a smaller specific dataset, can also be useful[2]. For example, researchers in India have used transfer learning to identify kidneys in ultrasound scans using only 45 training examples. It is a helpful step towards generalisation: transferring knowledge also means improving generalisation to the new task, even with limited data being available. This is in addition to transfer learning reducing training time and computational resources needed.

A further technical development is the use of synthetic data. Andrew Ng gives the example of trying to detect defects in smartphone casings and finding the model performing poorly on pit marks. An option to improve performance would be to generate synthetic data specifically for this category of error. Researchers have proven that it is possible to produce realistic synthetic data representative of UK primary care data[3]. They used an approach of integrating outlier analysis with graphical modelling and resampling to achieve outcomes that were close to ground truth data in terms of features distributions and dependencies, and a low risk of generating data that is identical to real patients.

Dr Sukhmeet Panesar says that compared to 10 years ago, and despite its limitations, he is becoming a huge advocate of synthetic data. He believes that it could 'provide a way for industry to access realistic NHS data, to really learn from the data, to show what it could do in terms of the different tools and the different methodologies'. He points to the innovative example of the German government publishing a Request for Proposal (RFP) in 2022 to develop a synthetic data set across the entire country. He believes synthetic data is a way to provide access to national data sets and 'create a fertile experimental innovation ground', which will help promote '1,000 flowers blooming rather than creating a process where only roses or tulips bloom'.

Johan Ordish and Russell Pearson also point out that synthetic data has potential value for regulation purposes, following adjustments to account for bias.

These datasets and environments that house them should be designed with a developer focus, rather than patient or clinician focused, Matt Bourne advises. This might mean easy access, clear documentation, software development kits (SDK) and APIs. This initiative could look at assets developed by others, for example Uber's ML platform infrastructure we discussed earlier.

There are questions about control and charges for access. Should it be freely available? Should the health systems charge for it? If so, how much? And how do they get some value back from it, should they receive IP and or a share of the company? Or should we pursue an idea similar to what Bart de Witte proposes with his licence, providing free access, with the condition that anything created needs to be shared in the same way? 'Learning data governance models' describes a feedback cycle to incorporate public opinions into data access requests[4]. The public are provided with outcomes of the data analysis and have the chance to provide feedback that will shape future decision making criteria.

Developing confidence and trust in the wider public

From a legal perspective, there is exploration that needs to be done around where accountability sits – whether it sits with the innovators who develop solutions, operators who procure them or end users that operate the solutions.

When thinking about the future of digital healthcare, artificial intelligence (AI) and its relations (machine learning and remote process automation) are often described as potential game changers in healthcare delivery. However, as Neville Young reminds us, algorithms, like any human, are not perfect, and that we need to start accepting this but also considering how indemnity works in these situations – do we think about this in a similar way we consider indemnity for clinicians, and if so, how does this work in healthcare system? If an algorithm provides a 'wrong' result, through no one's fault, we need to act proportionately ('not throw the baby out with the bathwater'). He likens this to not dismissing a clinician every time a genuine mistake occurs but instead using these as learning opportunities to improve overall care. Algorithms are not legally allowed to make fully autonomous decisions in healthcare, and that if we want to move towards that, as well as changing primary legislation in the UK, Neville sees indemnity is an area to develop further.

There also needs to be wider legal protection for patients. As a high level comparison, consider the laws recently implemented in China covering algorithmic discrimination[5]. Companies will be banned from using personal information to exploit users by charging different prices for the same product or service (for example, a user who more often uses luxury rides on a ride hailing app being charged higher prices for the same ride). While not directly related to healthcare, this provides an example of the thinking countries need to do to minimise algorithmic harm.

On a related note is how to identify and address ethical considerations related to developing AI in healthcare. NHS England has collaborated with the Ada Lovelace Institute to develop an innovative pilot to support innovators assess the possible risks and biases of AI systems to patients and the public, especially minority groups[6]. These Algorithmic Impact Assessments (AIAs) will be trailed with a number of NHS AI Lab initiatives and used as part of the process to approve access to the National Covid-19 Chest Imaging Database (NCCID) and the proposed National Medical Imaging Platform (NMIP) datasets.

Johan Ordish and Russell Pearson suggest three key areas for improving regulation. First, is providing ethical access to high quality test beds. They explain that access to good data can translate to safety. Second, that regulation is fit for purpose. For example, having seamless processes across various assurance processes (for example, the Digital Technology Assessment Criteria or DTAC for digital health solutions) so that medical device requirements are incremental to DTAC requirements, are not duplicating processes and asks from innovators. Third, is translating the general medical device regulations to suit AI. For example, assuring the process by which the innovator makes a change to the solution (rather than the change itself) to strike the balance between assuring changes and making the change in a timely manner to deliver benefits to patients. The team is working with these initiatives and with other regulatory and compliance organisations in a programme called the 'Software and AI as a Medical Device Change Programme'[7].

Clíodhna Ní Ghuidhir is currently heading up the multi-agency advice service (MAAS) at NICE. MAAS brings together four organisations: NICE, Medicines and Healthcare products Regulatory Agency (MHRA), Health Research Authority (HRA), and the Care Quality Commission (CQC). These four groups provide more holistic regulatory advice for developers and adopters of AI technologies[8]. Clíodhna explains that MAAS was set up to span the work of the four organisations to 'join up the regulatory and evaluation pathway for AI and data driven tech and also to present that information in a way that's going to be user friendly and easy to digest'. It is expected that it will be a single online platform providing clear guidance on what must be done when, including the requirements that are essential.

MAAS enables more streamlined working, just by actually working together. 'If you have people who are consistently working together on understanding what the overall regulatory pathway is and therefore somebody gets a tricky issue which interacts with more than one regulator, they come together to articulate that and to work it through'. As well as mapping the end to end regulatory pathway, she says, they are doing policy work together to enable greater cohesiveness.

Central IG guidance and templates, as Barry Moult advocates, provide a unified view on risks and mitigations, and will be very useful. Neville points out similarities to when the National Institute for Health Research (NIHR) reviewed the ethics system 10 years ago (when you had to get ethics approval for every single organisation) and harmonised the requirements with the Health Research Authority (HRA), who now issue one ethical approval for a program.

In terms of validation, there is work that can be done to provide central guidance and methodologies that standardise activities at a local level and prevent duplication. When asked about areas within AI research where they should be more focus, Harshana Liyanage explains that 'there is more than enough work on new AI methodologies and often the challenge is finding the right method, weighing up the pros and cons'. He elaborates that newer algorithms, which may not be tested, require testing and that more research into methodologies that can make validation workflows more efficient would be useful.

Evaluation of the performance of models using data from the National COVID-19 Chest Imaging Database (NCCID) has provided a blueprint for evaluating the robustness of AI models[9]. The collaborative team conducted validation of five AI models developed using NCCID data by using proof of concept processes. The validation process assessed how the models performed with different patient groups and also assessed how the algorithm responds to changes in the underlying data, which will be helpful to reduce bias in the models.

It is also important to encourage and incentivise appropriate engagement and inclusivity. For example, to include and assess patient public involvement within grant applications and when evaluating solutions to procure. From an inclusivity perspective, the required emphasis must be placed and expected outcomes appropriately assessed to ensure that the solution does not increase health inequality and wherever possible helps reduce it.

Having the right people to support

To overcome the issue of healthcare professionals not having adequate capacity and headspace to engage with and support AI projects and tools, additional investment must be allocated (either on a permanent basis or on a project by project basis as part of the investment required).

Dr Neil Paul explains that relying on individual GP practices who are busy with day to day activities and clinical champions' goodwill is not a sustainable solution. He suggests the NHS needs a 'more formal innovation adoption system to include dedicated (funded) time for clinicians to adopt innovation and for this to be embedded into existing contractual mechanisms within primary care'. He explains that creating an early adoption panel consisting of interested GPs like himself and also funding supernumerary GP posts that can support the change management required could help. Neil thinks that could also enable 'clinical champions to spend time understanding more about what's out there, become subject matter experts and have the time to embed change by working on the ground at the various practices'.

Yosef Safi Harb agrees that appropriate budget allocations are required and also suggests that investing in resources such as project managers that can perform some of the preparation and administrative tasks will free up valuable clinician time.

Dr Sukhmeet Panesar proposes that AI centres of excellence (or 'AI factories') at a regional level could help with more widespread adoption. He thinks they could help regional ecosystems bringing together academia, industry, and the NHS to create a test bed for AI. He doesn't believe that it doesn't need to be 'a large building called the AI Center of Excellence' but more a 'virtual bringing together of partners to help you think about how you create an AI product from inception to actually something that you could commercialise'.

There is also the need to create, develop or promote specific roles with defined career paths (and entry points). First, are data analyst roles. Second, are hybrid clinical and data roles such as those of Dr Vishnu Chandrabalan and Dr Matt Stammers. Third, are dedicated innovation roles at regional level, for example at ICS level. Neville

Young explains that as we emerge from the Covid-19 pandemic that our risk appetite around innovation needs to evolve. During the pandemic, the system had to take some risks with innovation to help with the immediate crisis. A lot of that innovation was successful, but some less so. Looking to the future of innovation in healthcare we still need to be able to take appropriate risks with innovation where the prize is to dramatically improve the care of patients. We shouldn't revert back to pre-Covid levels of risk aversion that meant it was a struggle to innovate at pace and scale in the NHS. Instead, he believes that having individuals responsible for and empowered to innovate at all levels in an organisation including at executive level is one of the important steps to achieving this balance.

Dr Sukhmeet Panesar explains that while we might not need a 'Royal College of AI' or setting of standards across everything, there needs to be a clear understanding of career paths in AI and strong sponsorship in the form of resources. He suggests the need, based on the different mindset and approach required for AI, for the role of a 'Chief AI officer' for the NHS. He explains that he is working with AphA (Association of professional healthcare analysts) to co-produce career paths for data analysts and a bespoke curriculum that is relevant to each grade (which then can be partly provided by industry and technology vendors in a meaningful way). When asked about roles, other than data analysts, for the successful development and implementation of AI, Sukhmeet points to data engineering, DevOps, product owner and knowledge management on the roadmap.

The other crucial element is to upskill, train and educate individuals so that they can engage and support effectively.

Sukhmeet explains that clinicians are a 'very, very important part in the army for change' due to their strong understanding of the front line. He suggests that adding AI knowledge means a 'complete package'. He suggests several options to make this happen, with the caveat that all have their challenges. As suggested by others, AI could be integrated into the clinical undergraduate curriculum.

Sukhmeet thinks there is potential to carve out dedicated time for clinicians to spend some of their time on AI and health technology related work. This is difficult, he acknowledges, when there is a clinical workforce that is in short supply, and it will take a lot of courage from hospital leadership. One more practical option he suggests is the creation of more 'out of program type experiences', for example clinicians taking a year out on an 'AI fellowship'. The difficulty, he sees, is what happens after the year, and how the clinicians will be integrated back into clinical practice while retaining an active role in AI, and whether because of his difficulty the clinicians will end up leaving the NHS to pursue careers in industry.

Paolo Melissa highlights the importance of more basic education and information. He explains that most clinicians don't have a clear understanding of the capabilities of AI and that when they hear AI, they think of a magic black box that can solve any problem.

Samantha Riley is the Deputy Director of Intensive Support at NHS England and Improvement, and works on supporting the recovery of the most challenged hospitals and regional healthcare systems. She helps people use data in a better way, for example moving away from RAG reports and pie charts to methods such as Statistical Process Control (SPC) charts, which offer a more accurate reflection of variances. She explains that Covid-19 provided her with the opportunity to repurpose the way her team delivered training, moving away from face to face meetings that took up a lot of travelling time to virtual training sessions. The team has also divided the training into smaller chunks so that individuals have a better chance of taking time out of their day job to attend. Samantha uses the example of the unsuccessful national mandating of the 'Perfect week' programme (where management would walk the shop floor to fix operational issues) to make the point that the maximum impact is when stakeholders buy into a methodology rather than it being forced upon them. Her team is now developing a Massive Open Online Course (MOOC) to support analysts to 'Make data count'.

Sukhmeet highlights that data literacy is another area he is focusing on, based on the experiences and feedback during Covid-19 of helping NHS management make the best of data insights. He is working in partnership with R2 data labs (a spin off from Rolls Royce) to 'develop a set of learning offerings, not for the analysts, but for customers of analytical services and specifically aimed at the senior leadership teams within the NHS'.

Online communities, like AnalystX[10] which was set up in response to the Covid-19 pandemic for analysts working in NHS England and Improvement, and has now grown to more than 17,000 members. Initiative such as this which brings together like-minded people to share ideas and provides with them a curated and trusted collection of information and learning resources will be very useful to support the development of data analysts.

Sukhmeet is the Senior Responsible Officer (SRO) for AnalystX and explains that he wants to get to a state where 'we have a national backlog of analytical questions' and the AnalystX community can say 'I have the skill set, I can work with X and Y to tackle that particular question. I can access the data. Let me go away, solve it, and then I'll add it back to the collective'.

Collaborations between the public and private sectors may also help. For example, the Health AI Partnership collaboration launched in 2021 between Duke, Mayo Clinic, UC Berkeley and the law firm DLA Piper aims to promote better understanding of AI and enable safer implementation of AI solutions in healthcare[11]. The initiative will help decision makers make informed decisions by providing them with robust evidence and tested guidelines.

Investment approach and funding mechanisms

Investment strategies at national level must strike the correct balance between backing moon shots (very ambitious projects) and tackling the most difficult problems, and backing proven solutions and quick wins. Maneesh Juneja describes two extreme narratives of AI he encounters. One of utopia, which 'leads to AI solving every problem in healthcare, where staff never experience burnout and patients always have the best possible outcomes' and 'Everything is going to be amazing, we just have to deploy it!' The other narrative is dystopian: this is going to lead to 'unfair algorithms, black box AI, unexplainable AI, greater inequalities in healthcare and it's going to lead to more private sector involvement'. 'We don't want any of this!' Maneesh suggests the need for a more balanced conversation. 'Let's be realistic about AI, what it can deliver in the near term, but where it fits within the overall strategy for healthcare and ultimately how we can retain humanity in healthcare'.

On a related note, we need to incentivise researchers to solve real world problems and to ensure they are spending time solving the 'right' problems. This is important because research focused on application is often looked down upon in academia[12] and does not fully consider the impact of the research (beyond how interesting or challenging the problem is from a technical perspective)[13].

Funding should also be made available across different stages of development. For example, projects such Paulo Melissa's would benefit from more easily accessible 'bridge' funding to support the continuing development of the solution and to maximise the investment already made.

Dr Sukhmeet Panesar provides food for thought by suggesting that healthcare systems like the NHS should 'start betting on certain key initiatives that we think will really work'. He explains that if there is an AI company that 'aligns with NHS values and going to make a difference to society' and needs some seed funding or further funding, that the NHS can create the appropriate commercial vehicle to co-invest. He further explains that while the NHS will 'not be in it for the money', it allows 'us to be partners at the table, and provide the enabling support it needs...And if they are a success, the money can be invested back into the NHS'.

Due consideration must be given to how solutions are funded following successful development and implementation. National frameworks that provide an easy, consistent, and transparent routes to procurement, along with confidence that the solutions have been evaluated, and are safe and effective, will be useful. Neville Young highlights the importance of considering mechanisms such as 'dynamic' procurement systems (DPS), which aligns better with the fast changing environment of AI digital solutions, and allows new solutions to be effectively 'added' on an ongoing basis, if they meet appropriate clinical, governance and safety standards, rather than only once every two or three years, which can be the case for some of the current frameworks in existence. He cites some of the good work supporting the rapid roll out of several remote monitoring solutions that utilised DPS principles and driven implemented by NHS England during Covid-19 as a good example[14].

With the narrow focus of AI, and fragmented solutions described earlier, and the resulting need for solutions to 'work together' for optimal outcomes, good frameworks and procurement vehicles must be structured to support buyers to consider the right 'mix' of solutions. Common data models and open data standards will enable the interoperability required for solutions to 'collaborate' effectively. To gain the required spread of the same standards, a delicate balance must be struck between 'enforce' and 'incentivise', also considering the amount of top down implementation required in setting direction versus the bottom up implementation required to gain buy in (middle-out approach to implementation)[15].

Maneesh Juneja makes the observation that 'we don't want to be doing too much top down control, but I think there needs to be, because it is such an emerging fluid space'. He thinks that 'there needs to be more control from the centre nationally to say, hey, these are the standards you need to adhere to' and to avoid situations where 'two hospitals in London are partnering or piloting with the same or different arms of the same US provider and nobody realises it'. It sometimes feels like the Wild West because each hospital is doing their own thing when it comes to piloting AI.

After procurement, topics to address include how much payment, whether they are outcome based (risk sharing with innovators) and how and who makes the payments. And how do we ensure we achieve the benefits we pay for? This includes aspects such as investment in benefits realisation, from establishing an accurate beeline to change management and tracking of benefits achieved.

* * *

Thank you for giving me the opportunity to tell you about the challenges healthcare is going to face, how AI can help, and a better way to develop and deploy AI into healthcare. I hope you found it useful and that you have identified helpful insights that you can apply in your work.

If you have any feedback on this book, want to discuss any ideas or if there is anything I can help with, please contact me via LinkedIn or email me at janak@unlockaiforhealth.com It would also help other potential readers if you could leave an online review. Thank you.

I truly believe AI can help improve how we deliver healthcare, and the lives of patients and their families. Let's work together to make that happen.

REFERENCES

Chapter 1

1. WHO. 2021. Ageing and health. [Online] [Accessed: 17 November 2021]. Available at: https://www.who.int/news-room/fact-sheets/detail/ageing-and-health

2. Williams, J.S. and Egede, L.E., 2016. The association between multimorbidity and quality of life, health status and functional disability. The American journal of the medical sciences, 352(1), pp.45-52.

3. Stafford et al. 2018. Briefing: Understanding the health care needs of people with multiple health conditions. [Online] [Accessed: 17 November 2021] Available at: https://www.health.org.uk/sites/default/files/upload/publications/2018/Understanding%20the%20health%20care%20needs%20of%20people%20with%20multiple%20health%20conditions.pdf

4. NHS England. 2022. Consultant-led Referral to Treatment Waiting Times Data 2021-22. [Online] [Accessed: 02 May 2022] Available at: https://www.england.nhs.uk/statistics/statistical-work-areas/rtt-waiting-times/rtt-data-2021-22/

5. Jain, A., Jain, P. and Aggarwal, S., 2020. SARS-CoV-2 impact on elective orthopaedic surgery: implications for post-pandemic recovery. The Journal of bone and joint surgery. American volume.

6. Cisternas, A.F., Ramachandran, R., Yaksh, T.L. and Nahama, A., 2020. Unintended consequences of COVID-19 safety measures on patients with chronic knee pain forced to defer joint replacement surgery. Pain Reports, 5(6).

7. WHO. 2021. Health workforce. [Online] {Accessed: 17 November 2021] Available at: https://www.who.int/health-topics/health-workforce#tab=tab_1

8. BMA. 2021. Pressures in general practice. [Online] [Accessed: 02 April 2022] Available at: https://www.bma.org.uk/advice-and-support/nhs-delivery-and-workforce/pressures/pressures-in-general-practice

9. American Hospital Association. 2021. Fact Sheet: Strengthening the Health Care Workforce. [Online] [Accessed: 20 November 2021] Available at: https://www.aha.org/fact-sheets/2021-05-26-fact-sheet-strengthening-health-care-workforce

10. Singh, H., Meyer, A.N. and Thomas, E.J., 2014. The frequency of diagnostic errors in outpatient care: estimations from three large observational studies involving US adult populations. BMJ quality & safety, 23(9), pp.727-731.

11. Cheraghi-Sohi, S., Holland, F., Singh, H., Danczak, A., Esmail, A., Morris, R.L., Small, N., Williams, R., de Wet, C., Campbell, S.M. and Reeves, D., 2021. Incidence, origins and avoidable harm of missed opportunities in diagnosis: longitudinal patient record review in 21 English general practices. BMJ Quality & Safety.

12. Hussain, F., Cooper, A., Carson-Stevens, A., Donaldson, L., Hibbert, P., Hughes, T. and Edwards, A., 2019. Diagnostic error in the emergency department: learning from national patient safety incident report analysis. BMC emergency medicine, 19(1), pp.1-9.

13. Elliott, R.A., Camacho, E., Jankovic, D., Sculpher, M.J. and Faria, R., 2021. Economic analysis of the prevalence and clinical and economic burden of medication error in England. BMJ Quality & Safety, 30(2), pp.96-105.

14. Topol, E., 2019. Deep medicine: how artificial intelligence can make healthcare human again. Hachette UK.

15. Irving, G., Neves, A.L., Dambha-Miller, H., Oishi, A., Tagashira, H., Verho, A. and Holden, J., 2017. International variations in primary care physician consultation time: a systematic review of 67 countries. BMJ open, 7(10), p.e017902.

16. Salisbury, H., 2019. Helen Salisbury: The 10 minute appointment. Bmj, 365

17. Salisbury, C., Procter, S., Stewart, K., Bowen, L., Purdy, S., Ridd, M., Valderas, J., Blakeman, T. and Reeves, D., 2013. The content of general practice consultations: cross-sectional study based on video recordings. British Journal of General Practice, 63(616), pp.e751-e759.

18. Beasley, J.W., Hankey, T.H., Erickson, R., Stange, K.C., Mundt, M., Elliott, M., Wiesen, P. and Bobula, J., 2004. How many problems do family physicians manage at each encounter? A WReN study. The Annals of Family Medicine, 2(5), pp.405-410.

19. Galant, R. 2012. Why we need a new kind of doctor. [Online] [Accessed: 17 November 2021] Available at: https://edition.cnn.com/2012/05/13/opinion/gawande-doctors/index.html

20. Gawande, A. 2010. The Velluvial Matrix. The New Yorker. (Jan. 2010).

21. Clark, L. 2012. Vinod Khosla: Machines will replace 80 percent of doctors. [Online] [Accessed: 17 November 2021] Available at: https://www.wired.co.uk/article/doctors-replaced-with-machines

22. Heaven, WD. 2021. Hundreds of AI tools have been built to catch covid. None of them helped. [Online] [Accessed: 17 November 2021] Available at: https://www.technologyreview.com/2021/07/30/1030329/machine-learning-ai-failed-covid-hospital-diagnosis-pandemic/

23. Beede, E., Baylor, E., Hersch, F., Iurchenko, A., Wilcox, L., Ruamviboonsuk, P. and Vardoulakis, L.M., 2020, April. A human-centered evaluation of a deep learning system deployed in clinics for the detection of diabetic retinopathy. In Proceedings of the 2020 CHI Conference on Human Factors in Computing Systems (pp. 1-12).

24. Wiggers, K. 2021. VCs invested over $75B in AI startups in 2020. [Online] [Accessed: 18 November 2021] Available at: https://venturebeat.com/2021/09/30/vcs-invested-over-75b-in-ai-startups-in-2020/

25. A. M. Turing (1950) Computing Machinery and Intelligence. Mind 49: 433-460.

26. BBC. 2014. Computer AI passes Turing test in 'world first' [Online] [Accessed: 17 November 2021] Available at: https://www.bbc.co.uk/news/technology-27762088

27. Pogue, D. 2018. Google's Duplex AI Scares Some People, but I Can't Wait for It to Become a Thing [Online] [Accessed: 17 November 2021] Available at: https://www.scientificamerican.com/article/googles-duplex-ai-scares-some-people-but-i-cant-wait-for-it-to-become-a-thing/

28. Floridi, L. and Chiriatti, M., 2020. GPT-3: Its nature, scope, limits, and consequences. Minds and Machines, 30(4), pp.681-694.

29. Living Internet. Dartmouth Artificial Intelligence (AI) Conference. [Online] [Accessed: 19 November 2021] Available at: https://www.livinginternet.com/i/ii_ai.htm

30. McCarthy, J. 2004. What is Artificial Intelligence? [Online] [Accessed: 17 November 2021] Available at: http://jmc.stanford.edu/articles/whatisai/whatisai.pdf

31. LeCun, Y., Bengio, Y. and Hinton, G., 2015. Deep learning. nature, 521(7553), pp.436-444.

Chapter 2

1. Davenport, T. and Kalakota, R., 2019. The potential for artificial intelligence in healthcare. Future healthcare journal, 6(2), p.94.

2. Bohr, A. and Memarzadeh, K., 2020. The rise of artificial intelligence in healthcare applications. In Artificial Intelligence in healthcare (pp. 25-60). Academic Press.

3. Shaheen, M.Y., 2021. Applications of Artificial Intelligence (AI) in healthcare: A review. ScienceOpen Preprints.

4. https://www.benevolent.com/what-we-do

5. https://healx.io/technology/

6. Spatharou, A et al. 2020. Transforming healthcare with AI: The impact on the workforce and organizations. [Online] [Accessed: 15 January 2022] Available at: https://www.mckinsey.com/industries/healthcare-systems-and-services/our-insights/transforming-healthcare-with-ai

7. Zhang, J., Whebell, S., Gallifant, J., Budhdeo, S., Mattie, H., Lertvittayakumjorn, P., del Pilar Lopez, M., Tiangco, B., Gichoya, J.W., Ashrafian, H. and Celi, L.A., 2021. An interactive dashboard to track themes, development maturity, and global equity in clinical artificial intelligence research. medRxiv.

8. FDA. 2022. Artificial Intelligence and Machine Learning (AI/ML)-Enabled Medical Devices. [Online] [Accessed: 19 January 2022]. Available at: https://www.fda.gov/medical-devices/software-medical-device-samd/artificial-intelligence-and-machine-learning-aiml-enabled-medical-devices

9. Arora, K, Sharma, V. 2020. India's top Artificial Intelligence Organizations in Healthcare. [Online] [Accessed: 15 January 2022]. Available at: https://innohealthmagazine.com/2020/innovation/top-artificial-intelligence-organizations-in-healthcare-in-india/

10. AdviseInc. 2020. Covid-19 PPE Tracker. [Online] [Accessed: 16 January 2022] Available at: https://www.hsj.co.uk/download?ac=3045377

11. Kumar, G., Basri, S., Imam, A.A., Khowaja, S.A., Capretz, L.F. and Balogun, A.O., 2021. Data Harmonization for Heterogeneous Datasets: A Systematic Literature Review. Applied Sciences, 11(17), p.8275.

12. Rosas, M.A., Bezerra, A.F.B. and Duarte-Neto, P.J., 2013. Use of artificial neural networks in applying methodology for allocating health resources. Revista de saude publica, 47(1), pp.128-136.

REFERENCES

13. Moyo, S., Doan, T.N., Yun, J.A. and Tshuma, N., 2018. Application of machine learning models in predicting length of stay among healthcare workers in underserved communities in South Africa. Human resources for health, 16(1), pp.1-9.

14. Lovell, T. 2022. British tech firm Faculty partners with NHS to forecast A&E admissions. [Online] [Accessed: 29 March 2022] Available at: https://www.healthcareitnews.com/news/emea/british-tech-firm-faculty-partners-nhs-forecast-ae-admissions

15. Ahmed, S., Nutt, C.T., Eneanya, N.D., Reese, P.P., Sivashanker, K., Morse, M., Sequist, T. and Mendu, M.L., 2021. Examining the potential impact of race multiplier utilization in estimated glomerular filtration rate calculation on African-American care outcomes. Journal of general internal medicine, 36(2), pp.464-471.

16. Keating, M. 2021. Capacity Command Center Celebrates 5 Years of Improving Patient Safety, Access. [Online][Accessed: 16 January 2022] Available at: https://www.hopkinsmedicine.org/news/articles/capacity-command-center-celebrates-5-years-of-improving-patient-safety-access

17. https://www.pinpointdatascience.com/

18. https://www.drdoctor.co.uk/

19. Austin-Morgan, T. 2021. How AI is transforming the NHS. [Online] [Accessed: 21 January 2022] Available at: https://www.newelectronics.co.uk/electronics-technology/how-ai-is-transforming-the-nhs-1/235075/

20. Helfinstein, S., Engl, E., Thomas, B.E., Natarajan, G., Prakash, P., Jain, M., Lavanya, J., Jagadeesan, M., Chang, R., Mangono, T. and Kemp, H., 2020. Understanding why at-risk population segments do not seek care for tuberculosis: a precision public health approach in South India. BMJ global health, 5(9), p.e002555.

21. FollowApp.care. 2022. Use Cases. [Online] [Accessed: 16 January 2022]. Available at: https://www.followapp.care/use-cases/

22. AllazoHealth. 2020. [Online] [Accessed: 16 January 2022] Available at https://allazohealth.com/

23. Bates, D.W., Levine, D., Syrowatka, A., Kuznetsova, M., Craig, K.J.T., Rui, A., Jackson, G.P. and Rhee, K., 2021. The potential of artificial intelligence to improve patient safety: a scoping review. NPJ digital medicine, 4(1), pp.1-8.

24. Zhao, M., Hoti, K., Wang, H., Raghu, A. and Katabi, D., 2021. Assessment of medication self-administration using artificial intelligence. Nature medicine, 27(4), pp.727-735.

25. https://healthy.io/

26. Jvion. 2022. Preventing Readmissions with Clinical AI. [Online] [Accessed: 16 January 2022] Available at: https://jvion.com/applications/readmissions-reduction/

27. Romero-Brufau, S., Wyatt, K.D., Boyum, P., Mickelson, M., Moore, M. and Cognetta-Rieke, C., 2020. Implementation of artificial intelligence-based clinical decision support to reduce hospital readmissions at a regional hospital. Applied Clinical Informatics, 11(04), pp.570-577.

28. eviCore. 2020. How Artificial Intelligence Can Make Hospital Administration More Efficient. [Online] [Accessed: 16 January 2022] Available at: https://www.evicore.com/insights/how-artificial-intelligence-can-make-hospital-administration-more-efficient

29. Infinx. 2022. See More Patients, Collect More Revenue. [Online] [Accessed: 16 January 2022] Available at: https://www.infinx.com/international

30. Wang, P., Berzin, T.M., Brown, J.R.G., Bharadwaj, S., Becq, A., Xiao, X., Liu, P., Li, L., Song, Y., Zhang, D. and Li, Y., 2019. Real-time automatic detection system increases colonoscopic polyp and adenoma detection rates: a prospective randomised controlled study. Gut, 68(10), pp.1813-1819.

31. Cedars-Sinai. 2022. Cedars-Sinai Taps Alexa for Smart Hospital Room Pilot [Online] [Accessed: 16 January 2021] Available at: https://www.cedars-sinai.org/newsroom/cedars-sinai-taps-alexa-for-smart-hospital-room-pilot/

32. Topol, E., 2019. Deep medicine: how artificial intelligence can make healthcare human again. Hachette UK.

33. Bennet, T. 2021. Chatbot offers real-time medication, symptom support for patients with cancer. [Online] [Accessed: 16 January 2022] Available at: https://www.healio.com/news/hematology-oncology/20210415/chatbot-offers-realtime-medication-symptom-support-for-patients-with-cancer

34. https://www.wysa.io/

35. Lomas, N. 2021. ifeel, another well-being platform that blends self-care tools with 1-2-1 therapy, scores $6.6M. [Online] [Accessed: 21 January 2022] Available at: https://techcrunch.com/2021/05/06/ifeel-another-well-being-platform-that-blends-self-care-tools-with-1-2-1-therapy-scores-6-6m/

36. https://oliveai.com/payers/clearinghouse

37. https://oliveai.com/providers/reimbursement-management

38. https://beamtree.com.au/

39. https://beamtree.com.au/news/international-growth-first-nhs-contracts/

40. Grover, D., Bauhoff, S. and Friedman, J., 2019. Using supervised learning to select audit targets in performance-based financing in health: An example from Zambia. PloS one, 14(1), p.e0211262.

41. Yokeru. 2022. Radius Connect24 - Automate Wellbeing Calls. [Online] {Accessed: 17 January 2022] Available at: https://www.yokeru.io

42. The Learning Healthcare Project. 2022. Learning Healthcare System. [Online] {Accessed: 17 January 2022] Available at: https://learninghealthcareproject.org/background/learning-healthcare-system/

43. https://www.ekohealth.com/

44. https://huma.com/hospital-at-home

45. Dabbah, M.A., Reed, A.B., Booth, A.T., Yassaee, A., Despotovic, A., Klasmer, B., Binning, E., Aral, M., Plans, D., Labrique, A.B. and Mohan, D., 2021. Machine learning approach to dynamic risk modelling of mortality in COVID-19: a UK Biobank study. arXiv preprint arXiv:2104.09226.

Chapter 3

1. Babylon. 2022. Babylon Again Delivers Significant Growth to Reach Over 440,000 Managed Lives Globally, After Signing New US Value-Based Care Agreements. [Online] [Accessed: 22 January 2022] Available at: https://ir.babylonhealth.com/news-events/press-releases/detail/64/babylon-again-delivers-significant-growth-to-reach-over#:~:text=%2D%2D(BUSINESS%20WIRE)%2D%2D%20Babylon,managed%20lives%20to%20over%20440%2C000.

2. Somauroo, J. 2020. Qure.ai Deploys AI Radiology Software In The Fight Against COVID-19. [Online] [Accessed: 28 January 2022] Available at: https://www.forbes.com/sites/jamessomauroo/2020/04/27/qureai-deploys-ai-radiology-software-in-the-fight-against-covid-19/?sh=65170d63607e

3. Building Better Healthcare. 2021. Artificial intelligence in the real world. [Online] [Accessed: 28 January 2022] Available at: https://www.buildingbetterhealthcare.com/news/article_page/Artificial_intelligence_in_the_real_world/174239

4. Nagaratnam, K., Harston, G., Flossmann, E., Canavan, C., Geraldes, R.C. and Edwards, C., 2020. Innovative use of artificial intelligence and digital communication in acute stroke pathway in response to COVID-19. Future Healthcare Journal, 7(2), p.169.

5. Sendak, M.P., Ratliff, W., Sarro, D., Alderton, E., Futoma, J., Gao, M., Nichols, M., Revoir, M., Yashar, F., Miller, C. and Kester, K., 2020. Real-world integration of a sepsis deep learning technology into routine clinical care: implementation study. JMIR medical informatics, 8(7), p.e15182.

6. Sendak, M., Elish, M.C., Gao, M., Futoma, J., Ratliff, W., Nichols, M., Bedoya, A., Balu, S. and O'Brien, C., 2020, January. "The human body is a black box" supporting clinical decision-making with deep learning. In Proceedings of the 2020 conference on fairness, accountability, and transparency (pp. 99-109).

7. Bedoya, A.D., Clement, M.E., Phelan, M., Steorts, R.C., O'Brien, C. and Goldstein, B.A., 2019. Minimal impact of implemented early warning score and best practice alert for patient deterioration. Critical care medicine, 47(1), p.49.

8. Landro, L. 2022. How Hospitals Are Using AI to Save Lives. [Online] [Accessed: 26 April 2022] Available at: https://www.wsj.com/articles/how-hospitals-are-using-ai-to-save-lives-11649610000

9. McKinsey. 2021. The state of AI in 2021. [Online] [Accessed: 22 January 2022] Available at: https://www.mckinsey.com/business-functions/mckinsey-analytics/our-insights/global-survey-the-state-of-ai-in-2021

10. Babitz, K. 2021. How Google, Uber, and Amazon Ensure High-Quality Data at Scale. [Online] [Accessed: 29 January 2022] Available at: https://medium.com/swlh/how-3-of-the-top-tech-companies-approach-data-quality-79c3146fd959

11. Valle, C.G., Queen, T.L., Martin, B.A., Ribisl, K.M., Mayer, D.K. and Tate, D.F., 2018. Optimizing tailored communications for health risk assessment: a randomized factorial experiment of the effects of expectancy priming, autonomy support, and exemplification. Journal of medical Internet research, 20(3), p.e7613.

12. Harris, D. 2012. Netflix analyzes a lot of data about your viewing habits. [Online] [Accessed: 23 January 20222]. Available at: https://gigaom.com/2012/06/14/netflix-analyzes-a-lot-of-data-about-your-viewing-habits/

13. Dye, M et al. 2020. Supporting content decision makers with machine learning. [Online] [Accessed: 23 January 2022] Available at: https://netflixtechblog.com/supporting-content-decision-makers-with-machine-learning-995b7b76006f

14. Orcan intelligence. 2018. How Netflix Uses Big Data. [Online] [Accessed: 23 January 2022] Available at: https://medium.com/swlh/how-netflix-uses-big-data-20b5419c1edf

15. Gomez-Uribe, C.A. and Hunt, N., 2015. The Netflix recommender system: Algorithms, business value, and innovation. ACM Transactions on Management Information Systems (TMIS), 6(4), pp.1-19.

16. Silberling, A. 2022. Netflix had its lowest year of subscriber growth since 2015. [Online] [Accessed: 22 January 2022] Available at: https://techcrunch.com/2022/01/20/netflix-q4-2021-results-subscriber-numbers/

17. https://companiesmarketcap.com/netflix/revenue/

18. Marr, B. 2022. How Amazon Uses Artificial Intelligence: The Flywheel Approach. [Online] [Accessed: 24 January 2022] Available at: https://bernardmarr.com/how-amazon-uses-artificial-intelligence-the-flywheel-approach/

19. Krysik, A. 2021. Amazon's Product Recommendation System In 2021: How Does The Algorithm Of The eCommerce Giant Work?. [Online] [Accessed: 24 January 2022]. Available at: https://recostream.com/blog/amazon-recommendation-system

20. MacKenzie, I et al. 2013. How retailers can keep up with consumers. [Online] [Accessed: 24 January 2022]. Available at: https://www.mckinsey.com/industries/retail/our-insights/how-retailers-can-keep-up-with-consumers

21. Boteanu, A. 2020. Why do you want that? (And who's it for?). [Online] [Accessed: 26 January 2022] Available at: https://www.amazon.science/blog/why-do-you-want-that-and-whos-it-for

22. Grasso, C. 2019. How Amazon Leverages Artificial Intelligence to Optimize Delivery. [Online] [Accessed: 26 January 2022] Available at: https://feedvisor.com/resources/amazon-shipping-fba/how-amazon-leverages-artificial-intelligence-to-optimize-delivery/

23. Curry, D. 2022. Amazon Statistics (2022). [Online] [Accessed: 23 January 2022]. Available at: https://www.businessofapps.com/data/amazon-statistics/

24. Macrotrends. 2022. Amazon Revenue 2006-2021 | AMZN. [Online] [Accessed: 23 January 2022]. Available at: https://www.macrotrends.net/stocks/charts/AMZN/amazon/revenue

25. Uber. 2021. Uber Announces Results for Third Quarter 2021. [Online] [Accessed: 26 January 2021] Available at: https://investor.uber.com/news-events/news/press-release-details/2021/Uber-Announces-Results-for-Third-Quarter-2021/

26. Koetsier, J. 2018. Uber Might Be The First AI-First Company, Which Is Why They 'Don't Even Think About It Anymore'. [Online] [Accessed: 26 January 2022] Available at: https://www.forbes.com/sites/johnkoetsier/2018/08/22/uber-might-be-the-first-ai-first-company-which-is-why-they-dont-even-think-about-it-anymore/?sh=59aa83005b62

27. Xu, C. 2020. How to be UBER successful at enterprise scale AI. [Online] [Accessed: 26 January 2022] Available at: https://digital.hbs.edu/platform-digit/submission/how-to-be-uber-successful-at-enterprise-scale-ai/

Chapter 4

1. Valeor, A et al. 2021. The business response to Covid-19 one year on: findings from the second wave of the CEP-CBI survey on technology adoption. [Online] [Accessed: 01 January 2022] Available at: https://cep.lse.ac.uk/pubs/download/cepcovid-19-024.pdf

2. Harvey Nash and KPMG. 2020. CIO Survey 2020. [Online] [Accessed: 01 January 2022] Available at: https://assets.kpmg/content/dam/kpmg/xx/pdf/2020/10/harvey-nash-kpmg-cio-survey-2020.pdf

3. Institute of Global Health Innovation & EY. 2021. Embracing digital: is COVID-19 the catalyst for lasting change? [Online] [Accessed: 01 January 2022] Available at: https://www.ey.com/en_gl/government-public-sector/embracing-digital-is-covid-19-the-catalyst-for-lasting-change

4. Bestsennyy, O et al. 2021. Telehealth: A quarter-trillion-dollar post-COVID-19 reality? [Online] [Accessed: 02 January 2022] Available at: https://www.mckinsey.com/industries/healthcare-systems-and-services/our-insights/telehealth-a-quarter-trillion-dollar-post-covid-19-reality

5. Gilbert, A.W., Billany, J.C., Adam, R., Martin, L., Tobin, R., Bagdai, S., Galvin, N., Farr, I., Allain, A., Davies, L. and Bateson, J., 2020. Rapid implementation of virtual clinics due to COVID-19: report and early evaluation of a quality improvement initiative. BMJ open quality, 9(2), p.e000985.

6. https://www.nhsbsa.nhs.uk/statistical-collections/general-pharmaceutical-services-england/general-pharmaceutical-services-england-201516-202021

7. Wickware, C. 2021. Online pharmacy dispensing volume grows by 45% in 2020, fuelled by COVID-19 pandemic. [Online] [Accessed: 02 January 2022] Available at: https://pharmaceutical-journal.com/article/news/online-pharmacy-dispensing-volume-grows-by-45-in-2020-fuelled-by-covid-19-pandemic

8. Horton, T et al. 2021. Securing a positive health care technology legacy from COVID-19. [Online] [Accessed: 02 January 2022] Available at: https://www.health.org.uk/publications/long-reads/securing-a-positive-health-care-technology-legacy-from-covid-19

9. Massoudi, B.L. and Sobolevskaia, D., 2021. Keep moving forward: health informatics and information management beyond the COVID-19 pandemic. Yearbook of Medical Informatics, 30(01), pp.075-083

10. Baum, S. 2021. The health tech and medtech investment landscape in the age of Covid-19. [Online] [Accessed: 02 January 2022] Available at: https://medcitynews.com/2021/10/the-health-tech-and-medtech-investment-landscape-in-the-age-of-covid-19/

11. NHSX. 2020. COVID-19 IG advice. [Online] [Accessed: 02 January 2022] Available at: https://www.nhsx.nhs.uk/information-governance/guidance/covid-19-ig-advice/

12. ICO. 2020. Data protection and coronavirus. [Online] [Accessed: 02 January 2022] Available at: https://ico.org.uk/about-the-ico/news-and-events/news-and-blogs/2020/03/data-protection-and-coronavirus/

13. Rapson, J. 2020. Funding for new tech to help covid-19 crisis revealed. [Online] [Accessed: 02 January 2022] Available at: https://www.hsj.co.uk/coronavirus/funding-for-new-tech-to-help-covid-19-crisis-revealed/7027209.article

14. Fiore, V. 2021. £1.4k for Scottish pharmacies that set up COVID-19 delivery service. [Online] [Accessed: 02 January 2022] Available at: https://www.chemistanddruggist.co.uk/CD006951/14k-for-Scottish-pharmacies-that-set-up-COVID19-delivery-service

15. Hawks, C et al. 2021. Q3 2021 digital health funding: To $20B and beyond! [Online] [Accessed: 02 January 2022] Available at: https://rockhealth.com/insights/q1-2021-funding-report-digital-health-is-all-grown-up/

16. NHSX. Procurement frameworks. [Online] [Accessed: 02 January 2022] Available at: https://www.nhsx.nhs.uk/key-tools-and-info/procurement-frameworks/

17. Hughes, O. 2022. Microsoft Teams to be rolled out across NHS in response to coronavirus. [Online] [Accessed: 02 January 2022] Available at:https://www.digitalhealth.net/2020/03/microsoft-teams-nhs-coronavirus/

18. Freedom of Information request from NHS Improvement. 2020. [Accessed: 02 January 2022] Available at:https://www.england.nhs.uk/wp-content/uploads/2020/07/FOI-Attend-Anywhere-system.pdf

19. Gillette, F. 2021. Budget 2021: NHS in England to receive £5.9bn to cut waiting lists. [Online] [Accessed: 02 January 2022] Available at: https://www.bbc.co.uk/news/uk-59030945

20. Welsh Government. 2021. £25m boost for digital services across Welsh NHS. [Online] [Accessed: 02 January 2022] Available at:https://gov.wales/ps25m-boost-digital-services-across-welsh-nhs

21. Landi, H. 2021. HHS doling out $80M to improve public health IT, COVID-19 data collection. [Online] [Accessed: 02 January 2022] Available at:https://www.fiercehealthcare.com/tech/hhs-doling-out-80m-to-improve-public-health-it-covid-19-data-collection

22. OECD. 2019. Fiscal challenges and inclusive growth in ageing societies. [Online] [Accessed: 27 December 2021] Available at: https://www.oecd.org/economy/ageing-inclusive-growth/

23. Wittenberg, R et al. 2019. Projections of older people with dementia and costs of dementia care in the United Kingdom,2019–2040. [Online] [Accessed: 01 January 2022] Available at: https://www.alzheimers.org.uk/sites/default/files/2019-11/cpec_report_november_2019.pdf

24. Turner, G. 2014. Introduction to Frailty, Fit for Frailty. [Online] [Accessed: 01 January 2022] Available at: https://www.bgs.org.uk/resources/introduction-to-frailty

25. Clegg, A., Young, J., Iliffe, S., Rikkert, M.O. and Rockwood, K., 2013. Frailty in elderly people. The lancet, 381(9868), pp.752-762

26. Siriwardhana, D.D., Hardoon, S., Rait, G., Weerasinghe, M.C. and Walters, K.R., 2018. Prevalence of frailty and prefrailty among community-dwelling older adults in low-income and middle-income countries: a systematic review and meta-analysis. BMJ open, 8(3), p.e018195.

27. Kingston, A., Robinson, L., Booth, H., Knapp, M., Jagger, C. and MODEM project, 2018. Projections of multi-morbidity in the older population in England to 2035: estimates from the Population Ageing and Care Simulation (PACSim) model. Age and ageing, 47(3), pp.374-380.

28. Jindai, K., Nielson, C.M., Vorderstrasse, B.A. and Quiñones, A.R., 2016. Peer reviewed: multimorbidity and functional limitations among adults 65 or older, NHANES 2005–2012. Preventing chronic disease, 13.

29. Barnett, K., Mercer, S.W., Norbury, M., Watt, G., Wyke, S. and Guthrie, B., 2012. Epidemiology of multimorbidity and implications for health care, research, and medical education: a cross-sectional study. The Lancet, 380(9836), pp.37-43.

30. Licchetta, M et al. 2016. Fiscal sustainability analytical paper: Fiscal sustainability and public spending on health. [Online] [Accessed: 01 January 2022] Available at: https://obr.uk/docs/dlm_uploads/Health-FSAP.pdf

31. Howdon, D. and Rice, N., 2018. Health care expenditures, age, proximity to death and morbidity: Implications for an ageing population. Journal of health economics, 57, pp.60-74.

32. Jayawardana, S., Cylus, J. and Mossialos, E., 2019. It's not ageing, stupid: why population ageing won't bankrupt health systems. European Heart Journal-Quality of Care and Clinical Outcomes, 5(3), pp.195-201.

33. Soley-Bori, M., Ashworth, M., Bisquera, A., Dodhia, H., Lynch, R., Wang, Y. and Fox-Rushby, J., 2021. Impact of multimorbidity on healthcare costs and utilisation: a systematic review of the UK literature. British Journal of General Practice, 71(702), pp.e39-e46.

34. Zhao, Y., Atun, R., Anindya, K., McPake, B., Marthias, T., Pan, T., van Heusden, A., Zhang, P., Duolikun, N. and Lee, J., 2021. Medical costs and out-of-pocket expenditures associated with multimorbidity in China: quantile regression analysis. BMJ global health, 6(2), p.e004042.

35. Bähler, C., Huber, C.A., Brüngger, B. and Reich, O., 2015. Multimorbidity, health care utilization and costs in an elderly community-dwelling population: a claims data based observational study. BMC health services research, 15(1), pp.1-12.

36. Griffith, L.E., Gruneir, A., Fisher, K., Panjwani, D., Gafni, A., Patterson, C., Markle-Reid, M. and Ploeg, J., 2019. Insights on multimorbidity and associated health service use and costs from three population-based studies of older adults in Ontario with diabetes, dementia and stroke. BMC health services research, 19(1), pp.1-11.

37. Comans, T.A., Peel, N.M., Hubbard, R.E., Mulligan, A.D., Gray, L.C. and Scuffham, P.A., 2016. The increase in healthcare costs associated with frailty in older people discharged to a post-acute transition care program. Age and ageing, 45(2), pp.317-320.

38. Centre for Medicare and Medicaid Services. 2010. Background: The Affordable Care Act's New Rules on Preventive Care. [Online] [Accessed: 01 January 2022] Available at: https://www.cms.gov/CCIIO/Resources/Fact-Sheets-and-FAQs/preventive-care-background#_ftn1

39. NHS England. 2019. NHS Long Term Plan. [Online] [Accessed: 01 January 2022] Available at: https://www.longtermplan.nhs.uk/

40. Institute for Public Policy Research. 2019. Ending the blame game The case for a new approach to public health and prevention. [Online] [Accessed: 01 January 2022] Available at: https://www.ippr.org/files/2019-06/public-health-and-prevention-june19.pdf

41. Australian Department of Health. 2019. Australia's Long Term National Health Plan. [Online] [Accessed: 01 January 2022] Available at: https://www.health.gov.au/resources/publications/australias-long-term-national-health-plan

42. WHO. 2021. Global strategy on digital health 2020-2025. [Online] [Accessed: 01 January 2022] Available at: https://www.who.int/docs/default-source/documents/gs4dhdaa2a9f352b0445bafbc79ca799dce4d.pdf

43. Abernethy, A. 2019. Statement on new steps to advance digital health policies that encourage innovation and enable efficient and modern regulatory oversight. [Online] [Accessed: 01 January 2022] Available at: https://www.fda.gov/news-events/press-announcements/statement-new-steps-advance-digital-health-policies-encourage-innovation-and-enable-efficient-and

44. Department of Health and Social Care. 2019. Health Secretary announces £250 million investment in artificial intelligence. [Online] [Accessed: 01 January 2022] Available at: https://www.gov.uk/government/news/health-secretary-announces-250-million-investment-in-artificial-intelligence

45. NHS England. Artificial Intelligence in Health and Care Award. [Online] [Accessed: 01 January 2022] Available at: https://www.england.nhs.uk/aac/what-we-do/how-can-the-aac-help-me/ai-award/

46. Golestaneh, L., Neugarten, J., Fisher, M., Billett, H.H., Gil, M.R., Johns, T., Yunes, M., Mokrzycki, M.H., Coco, M., Norris, K.C. and Perez, H.R., 2020. The association of race and COVID-19 mortality. EClinicalMedicine, 25, p.100455.

47. Collins Sr, et al. 2020. An Early Look at the Potential Implications of the COVID-19 Pandemic for Health Insurance Coverage. [Online] [Accessed: 02 January 2022] Available at:https://www.commonwealthfund.org/publications/issue-briefs/2020/jun/implications-covid-19-pandemic-health-insurance-survey

48. NHS England. 2021. Consultant-led Referral to Treatment Waiting Times Data 2021-22. [Online] [Accessed: 02 January 2022] Available at:https://www.england.nhs.uk/statistics/statistical-work-areas/rtt-waiting-times/rtt-data-2021-22/

49. Kulkarni, K., Shah, R., Armaou, M., Leighton, P., Mangwani, J. and Dias, J., 2021. What can we learn from the experiences and expectations of patients on growing waiting lists for planned care in the COVID-19 pandemic?. Bone & Joint Open, 2(8), pp.583-593.

50. Patel, K., Chapman, R., Gill, R. and Richards, J., 2021. Ensuring an equitable recovery for the NHS. bmj, 375.

51. Department of Health and Social Care. 2021. Additional £5.4 billion for NHS COVID-19 response over next 6 months. [Online] [Accessed: 02 January 2022] Available at:https://www.gov.uk/government/news/additional-54-billion-for-nhs-covid-19-response-over-next-six-months

52. Health Foundation. 2020. New analysis reveals daunting scale of financial challenge facing health and care post-COVID. [Online] [Accessed: 02 January 2022] Available at: https://www.health.org.uk/news-and-comment/news/new-analysis-reveals-scale-of-financial-challenge-facing-health-care-post-covid

53. Kurowski, C et al. 2021. From Double Shock to Double Recovery : Implications and Options for Health Financing in the Time of COVID-19. [Online] [Accessed: 02 January 2022] Available at:https://openknowledge.worldbank.org/bitstream/handle/10986/35298/From-Double-Shock-to-Double-Recovery-Implications-and-Options-for-Health-Financing-in-The-Time-of-COVID-19.pdf?sequence=8

54. Schumann, J. 2021. How Health Care In The U.S. May Change After COVID: An Optimist's Outlook. [Online] [Accessed: 02 January 2022] Available at:https://www.npr.org/sections/health-shots/2021/05/13/996233365/how-health-care-in-the-u-s-may-change-after-covid-an-optimists-outlook?t=1637966150560&t=1640712400356

55. Horton, T et al. 2021. Securing a positive health care technology legacy from COVID-19. [Online] [Accessed: 02 January 2022] Available at: https://www.health.org.uk/publications/long-reads/securing-a-positive-health-care-technology-legacy-from-covid-19

56. Rock Health. 2021. Rock Weekly. [Online] [Accessed: 02 January 2022] Available at: https://mailchi.mp/70c4e8f7af49/bricks-and-clicks-converge?e=42a0b67fd2

57. Litchfield, I., Shukla, D. and Greenfield, S., 2021. Impact of COVID-19 on the digital divide: a rapid review. BMJ open, 11(10), p.e053440.

58. Hospify. 2022. Hospify platform to be closed on 31st January 2022. [Online] [Accessed: 02 January 2022] Available at: https://www.hospify.com/news/2021/12/15/hospify-to-close-on-31st-january-2022

59. GSK. 2020. COVID-19 prompts increased focus on self-care. [Online] [Accessed: 02 January 2022] Available at: https://www.gsk.com/en-gb/media/press-releases/covid-19-prompts-increased-focus-on-self-care-with-europeans-taking-their-health-more-seriously-to-relieve-pressure-on-healthcare-systems/

60. Kearney, M et al. 2021. Post-COVID recovery: proactive care, self care and CVD prevention. [Online] [Accessed: 02 January 2022] Available at: https://uclpartners.com/blog-post/post-covid-recovery-proactive-care-self-care-and-cvd-prevention/

61. Zhao, M., Wasfy, J.H. and Singh, J.P., 2020. Sensor-aided continuous care and self-management: implications for the post-COVID era. The Lancet Digital Health, 2(12), pp.e632-e634.

62. Charles, A. 2021. The road to renewal: five priorities for health and care. [Online] [Accessed: 02 January 2022] Available at: https://www.independent.co.uk/news/health/nhs-mass-staff-shortage-christmas-b1981961.html

63. Giordano, C. 2021. NHS staff 'in despair' amid mass staff shortages over Christmas. [Online] [Accessed: 02 January 2022] Available at:https://www.independent.co.uk/news/health/nhs-mass-staff-shortage-christmas-b1981961.html

64. Executive Office of Labor and Workforce Development. 2021. Harvard Project on Workforce and Massachusetts Healthcare Collaborative Release Report on COVID-19's Impact on the Healthcare Workforce. [Accessed: 02 January 2022] Available at:https://www.mass.gov/news/harvard-project-on-workforce-and-massachusetts-healthcare-collaborative-release-report-on-covid-19s-impact-on-the-healthcare-workforce

65. BMA. 2021. £160m to treat millions on hospital waiting lists is nowhere near enough and the plans fail to acknowledge an exhausted workforce, says BMA. [Online] [Accessed: 02 January 2022] Available at:https://www.bma.org.uk/bma-media-centre/160m-to-treat-millions-on-hospital-waiting-lists-is-nowhere-near-enough-and-the-plans-fail-to-acknowledge-an-exhausted-workforce-says-bma

Chapter 5

1. Lie, D. 2012. Vinod Khosla: Technology Will Replace 80 Percent of Docs. [Online] [Accessed: 30 January 2022] Available at: https://thehealthcareblog.com/blog/2012/08/31/vinod-khosla-technology-will-replace-80-percent-of-docs/

2. Powell, A. 2020. AI revolution in medicine. [Online] [Accessed: 30 January 2022] Available at: https://news.harvard.edu/gazette/story/2020/11/risks-and-benefits-of-an-ai-revolution-in-medicine/

3. https://squareup.com/

4. Ben-Israel, D., Jacobs, W.B., Casha, S., Lang, S., Ryu, W.H.A., de Lotbiniere-Bassett, M. and Cadotte, D.W., 2020. The impact of machine learning on patient care: a systematic review. Artificial intelligence in medicine, 103, p.101785.

5. European Commission. 2021. Study on eHealth, Interoperability of Health Data and Artificial Intelligence for Health and Care in the European Union. [Online] [Accessed: 30 January 2022] Available at: https://ec.europa.eu/newsroom/dae/redirection/document/80948

6. Young, A.T., Amara, D., Bhattacharya, A. and Wei, M.L., 2021. Patient and general public attitudes towards clinical artificial intelligence: a mixed methods systematic review. The Lancet Digital Health, 3(9), pp.e599-e611.

7. Pheby, C. 2021. RoboDoc: Which health services would Brits be willing to receive from an AI? [Online] [Accessed: 30 January 2022] Available at: https://yougov.co.uk/topics/health/articles-reports/2021/04/22/robodoc-which-health-services-would-brits-be-willi

8. NHS Digital. 2021. What we mean by digital inclusion. [Online] [Accessed: 30 January 2022] Available at: https://digital.nhs.uk/about-nhs-digital/our-work/digital-inclusion/what-digital-inclusion-is

9. Ofcom. 2021. Digital divide narrowed by pandemic, but around 1.5m homes remain offline. [Online] [Accessed: 30 January 2022] Available at: https://www.ofcom.org.uk/about-ofcom/latest/media/media-releases/2021/digital-divide-narrowed-but-around-1.5m-homes-offline

10. Na, L., Yang, C., Lo, C.C., Zhao, F., Fukuoka, Y. and Aswani, A., 2018. Feasibility of reidentifying individuals in large national physical activity data sets from which protected health information has been removed with use of machine learning. JAMA network open, 1(8), pp.e186040-e186040.

11. Aggarwal, M., Gingras, C. and Deber, R., 2021. Artificial Intelligence in Healthcare from a Policy Perspective. In Multiple Perspectives on Artificial Intelligence in Healthcare (pp. 53-64). Springer, Cham.

12. Pascal, P. 2015. Google Photos identified two black people as 'gorillas'. [Online] [Accessed: 30 January 2022] Available at: https://mashable.com/archive/google-photos-black-people-gorillas#M.3Be4dBfuqB

13. Vincent, J. 2016. Twitter taught Microsoft's AI chatbot to be a racist asshole in less than a day. [Online] [Accessed: 20 January 2022] Available at: https://www.theverge.com/2016/3/24/11297050/tay-microsoft-chatbot-racist

14. Reuters. 2016. U.S. Opens Investigation After Fatal Crash in Tesla's Autopilot Mode. [Online] [Accessed: 30 January 2022] Available at: https://www.entrepreneur.com/article/278454

15. Evans, W. 2021. Amazon's Dark Secret: It Has Failed to Protect Your Data. [Online] [Accessed: 26 March 2022] Available at: https://www.wired.com/story/amazon-failed-to-protect-your-data-investigation/

16. Hern, A. 2017. Royal Free breached UK data law in 1.6m patient deal with Google's DeepMind. [Online] [Accessed: 30 January 2022] Available at: https://www.theguardian.com/technology/2017/jul/03/google-deepmind-16m-patient-royal-free-deal-data-protection-act

17. Suleyman, M, King. D. 2017. The Information Commissioner, the Royal Free, and what we've learned. [Online] [Accessed: 30 January 2022] Available at: https://deepmind.com/blog/announcements/ico-royal-free

18. BBC. 2021. DeepMind faces legal action over NHS data use. [Online] [Accessed: 30 January 2022] Available at: https://www.bbc.co.uk/news/technology-58761324

19. Lu, D. 2019. Creating an AI can be five times worse for the planet than a car. [Online]. [Accessed: 29 March 2022] Available at: https://www.newscientist.com/article/2205779-creating-an-ai-can-be-five-times-worse-for-the-planet-than-a-car/

20. Baxter, G. and Sommerville, I., 2011. Socio-technical systems: From design methods to systems engineering. Interacting with computers, 23(1), pp.4-17.

21. Hao, K. 2020. Doctors are using AI to triage covid-19 patients. The tools may be here to stay. [Online] [Accessed: 28 January 2022] Available at:https://www.technologyreview.com/2020/04/23/1000410/ai-triage-covid-19-patients-health-care/

22. Somauroo, J. 2020. Qure.ai Deploys AI Radiology Software In The Fight Against COVID-19. [Online] [Accessed: 28 January 2022] Available at: https://www.forbes.com/sites/jamessomauroo/2020/04/27/qureai-deploys-ai-radiology-software-in-the-fight-against-covid-19/?sh=65170d63607e

23. Richardson, J.P., Smith, C., Curtis, S., Watson, S., Zhu, X., Barry, B. and Sharp, R.R., 2021. Patient apprehensions about the use of artificial intelligence in healthcare. NPJ digital medicine, 4(1), pp.1-6.

24. Jacobs, M., Pradier, M.F., McCoy, T.H., Perlis, R.H., Doshi-Velez, F. and Gajos, K.Z., 2021. How machine-learning recommendations influence clinician treatment selections: the example of antidepressant selection. Translational psychiatry, 11(1), pp.1-9.

25. Ardila, D., Kiraly, A.P., Bharadwaj, S., Choi, B., Reicher, J.J., Peng, L., Tse, D., Etemadi, M., Ye, W., Corrado, G. and Naidich, D.P., 2019. End-to-end lung cancer screening with three-dimensional deep learning on low-dose chest computed tomography. Nature medicine, 25(6), pp.954-961.

26. Oakden-Rayner, L., Gale, W., Bonham, T.A., Lungren, M.P., Carneiro, G., Bradley, A.P. and Palmer, L.J., 2022. Validation and algorithmic audit of a deep learning system for the detection of proximal femoral fractures in patients in the emergency department: a diagnostic accuracy study. The Lancet Digital Health.

27. Warren, L.R., Clarke, J., Arora, S. and Darzi, A., 2019. Improving data sharing between acute hospitals in England: an overview of health record system distribution and retrospective observational analysis of inter-hospital transitions of care. BMJ open, 9(12), p.e031637.

28. https://www.iorahealth.com/

29. Sendak, M.P., Balu, S. and Schulman, K.A., 2017. Barriers to achieving economies of scale in analysis of EHR data. Applied clinical informatics, 8(03), pp.826-831.

30. Bloom, B.M., Pott, J., Thomas, S., Gaunt, D.R. and Hughes, T.C., 2021. Usability of electronic health record systems in UK EDs. Emergency Medicine Journal, 38(6), pp.410-415.

31. Obermeyer, Z., Powers, B., Vogeli, C. and Mullainathan, S., 2019. Dissecting racial bias in an algorithm used to manage the health of populations. Science, 366(6464), pp.447-453.

32. Kelly, C.J., Karthikesalingam, A., Suleyman, M., Corrado, G. and King, D., 2019. Key challenges for delivering clinical impact with artificial intelligence. BMC medicine, 17(1), pp.1-9.

33. Kim, D.W., Jang, H.Y., Kim, K.W., Shin, Y. and Park, S.H., 2019. Design characteristics of studies reporting the performance of artificial intelligence algorithms for diagnostic analysis of medical images: results from recently published papers. Korean journal of radiology, 20(3), pp.405-410.

34. Vickers, A.J., Cronin, A.M., Elkin, E.B. and Gonen, M., 2008. Extensions to decision curve analysis, a novel method for evaluating diagnostic tests, prediction models and molecular markers. BMC medical informatics and decision making, 8(1), pp.1-17.

35. van der Veer, S.N., Riste, L., Cheraghi-Sohi, S., Phipps, D.L., Tully, M.P., Bozentko, K., Atwood, S., Hubbard, A., Wiper, C., Oswald, M. and Peek, N., 2021. Trading off accuracy and explainability in AI decision-making: findings from 2 citizens' juries. Journal of the American Medical Informatics Association, 28(10), pp.2128-2138.

36. HIPPA journal. 2021. Largest Healthcare Data Breaches of 2021. [Online] [Accessed: 05 January 2022] Available at: https://www.hipaajournal.com/largest-healthcare-data-breaches-of-2021/

37. Mirsky, Y., Mahler, T., Shelef, I. and Elovici, Y., 2019. {CT-GAN}: Malicious Tampering of 3D Medical Imagery using Deep Learning. In 28th USENIX Security Symposium (USENIX Security 19) (pp. 461-478).

38. Hippisley-Cox, J., Coupland, C.A., Mehta, N., Keogh, R.H., Diaz-Ordaz, K., Khunti, K., Lyons, R.A., Kee, F., Sheikh, A., Rahman, S. and Valabhji, J., 2021. Risk prediction of covid-19 related death and hospital admission in adults after covid-19 vaccination: national prospective cohort study. bmj, 374.

39. Medeiros, J. 2021.How tech is changing healthcare. [Online] [Accessed: 29 Janaury 2022] Available at: https://www.wired.co.uk/article/future-health-trends

40. Heaven, WD. 2021. Hundreds of AI tools have been built to catch covid. None of them helped. [Online] [Accessed: 29 January 2022] Available at: https://www.technologyreview.com/2021/07/30/1030329/machine-learning-ai-failed-covid-hospital-diagnosis-pandemic/

41. Wynants, L., Van Calster, B., Collins, G.S., Riley, R.D., Heinze, G., Schuit, E., Bonten, M.M., Dahly, D.L., Damen, J.A., Debray, T.P. and De Jong, V.M., 2020. Prediction models for diagnosis and prognosis of covid-19: systematic review and critical appraisal. bmj, 369.

42. Roberts, M., Driggs, D., Thorpe, M., Gilbey, J., Yeung, M., Ursprung, S., Aviles-Rivero, A.I., Etmann, C., McCague, C., Beer, L. and Weir-McCall, J.R., 2021. Common pitfalls and recommendations for using machine learning to detect and prognosticate for COVID-19 using chest radiographs and CT scans. Nature Machine Intelligence, 3(3), pp.199-217.

Chapter 6

1. Feldman, K., Duncan, R.G., Nguyen, A., Cook-Wiens, G., Elad, Y., Nuckols, T. and Pevnick, J.M., 2022. Will Apple devices' passive atrial fibrillation detection prevent strokes? Estimating the proportion of high-risk actionable patients with real-world user data. Journal of the American Medical Informatics Association.

2. UK National Screening Committee. 2021. The pros and cons of screening. [Online] [Accessed: 06 May 2022] Available at: https://www.gov.uk/guidance/the-pros-and-cons-of-screening

3. Woolhandler, S. and Himmelstein, D.U., 2014. Administrative work consumes one-sixth of US physicians' working hours and lowers their career satisfaction. International Journal of Health Services, 44(4), pp.635-642.

4. Wang, D., Khosla, A., Gargeya, R., Irshad, H. and Beck, A.H., 2016. Deep learning for identifying metastatic breast cancer. arXiv preprint arXiv:1606.05718.

5. https://www.ohdsi.org/data-standardization/the-common-data-model/

6. Hemming, K., Haines, T.P., Chilton, P.J., Girling, A.J. and Lilford, R.J., 2015. The stepped wedge cluster randomised trial: rationale, design, analysis, and reporting. Bmj, 350.

7. Oliver, N., Barber, X., Roomp, K. and Roomp, K., 2020. Assessing the impact of the COVID-19 pandemic in Spain: Large-scale, online, self-reported population survey. Journal of medical Internet research, 22(9), p.e21319.

8. Nusca, A. 2013. After a year of medical school, IBM's Watson passes first milestone. [Online] [Accessed: 10 February 2022] Available at: https://www.zdnet.com/article/after-a-year-of-medical-school-ibms-watson-passes-first-milestone/

9. Lohr, S. 2021. What Ever Happened to IBM's Watson?. [Online] [Accessed: 08 February 2022] Available at: https://www.nytimes.com/2021/07/16/technology/what-happened-ibm-watson.html

10. Schlingman, J.P. 2019. Artificial Intelligence Systems, Like IBM's Watson, Continue to Underperform When Compared to Oncologists and Anatomic Pathologists. [Online] [Accessed:11 February 2022] Available at: https://www.darkdaily.com/2019/08/21/artificial-intelligence-systems-like-ibms-watson-continue-to-underperform-when-compared-to-oncologists-and-anatomic-pathologists/

11. Peck, A.D. 2018. IBM's Watson Not Living Up to Hype, Wall Street Journal and Other Media Report; 'Dr. Watson' Has Yet to Show It Can Improve Patient Outcomes or Accurately Diagnose Cancer. [Online] [Accessed: 11 February 2022] Available at: https://www.darkdaily.com/2018/09/21/ibms-watson-not-living-up-to-hype-wall-street-journal-and-other-media-report-dr-watson-has-yet-to-show-it-can-improve-patient-outcomes-or-accurately-diagnose-cancer/

12. Miliard, M. 2021. IBM sale of Watson Health could enable renewed focus on cloud growth. [Online] [Accessed: 10 February 2022] Available at: https://www.healthcareitnews.com/news/ibm-sale-watson-health-could-enable-renewed-focus-cloud-growth

13. Advisory Board. 2021. 10 years ago, IBM's Watson threatened to disrupt health care. What happened? [Online] [Accessed: 11 February 2022] Available at: https://www.advisory.com/daily-briefing/2021/07/21/ibm-watson

14. Ross, C, Swetlitz, I. 2017. IBM pitched its Watson supercomputer as a revolution in cancer care. It's nowhere close. [Online] [Accessed: 11 February 2022] Available at: https://www.statnews.com/2017/09/05/watson-ibm-cancer/

15. IBM. 2022. Francisco Partners to Acquire IBM's Healthcare Data and Analytics Assets. [Online] [Accessed: 10 February 2022] Available at: https://newsroom.ibm.com/2022-01-21-Francisco-Partners-to-Acquire-IBMs-Healthcare-Data-and-Analytics-Assets

Chapter 7

1. Pierson, E., Cutler, D.M., Leskovec, J., Mullainathan, S. and Obermeyer, Z., 2021. An algorithmic approach to reducing unexplained pain disparities in underserved populations. Nature Medicine, 27(1), pp.136-140.

2. Sullivan, H.R, Schweikart, S.J. 2019. Are Current Tort Liability Doctrines Adequate for Addressing Injury Caused by AI? [Online] [Accessed: 20 February 2022] Available at: https://journalofethics.ama-assn.org/article/are-current-tort-liability-doctrines-adequate-addressing-injury-caused-ai/2019-02

Chapter 8

1. Greenhalgh, T., Wherton, J., Papoutsi, C., Lynch, J., Hughes, G., Hinder, S., Fahy, N., Procter, R. and Shaw, S., 2017. Beyond adoption: a new framework for theorizing and evaluating nonadoption, abandonment, and challenges to the scale-up, spread, and sustainability of health and care technologies. Journal of medical Internet research, 19(11), p.e8775.

2. Higgins, D. and Madai, V.I., 2020. From bit to bedside: a practical framework for artificial intelligence product development in healthcare. Advanced intelligent systems, 2(10), p.2000052.

3. Higgins, D.C., 2021. OnRAMP for Regulating Artificial Intelligence in Medical Products. Advanced Intelligent Systems, 3(11), p.2100042.

4. Reddy, S., Rogers, W., Makinen, V.P., Coiera, E., Brown, P., Wenzel, M., Weicken, E., Ansari, S., Mathur, P., Casey, A. and Kelly, B., 2021. Evaluation framework to guide implementation of AI systems into healthcare settings. BMJ health & care informatics, 28(1).

5. Sendak, M., Elish, M.C., Gao, M., Futoma, J., Ratliff, W., Nichols, M., Bedoya, A., Balu, S. and O'Brien, C., 2020, January. "The human body is a black box" supporting clinical decision-making with deep learning. In Proceedings of the 2020 conference on fairness, accountability, and transparency (pp. 99-109).

6. Scott, I., Carter, S. and Coiera, E., 2021. Clinician checklist for assessing suitability of machine learning applications in healthcare. BMJ Health & Care Informatics, 28(1).

7. Joshi, I., Morley, J. 2019. Artificial Intelligence: How to get it right. Putting policy into practice for safe data-driven innovation in health and care. [Online] [Accessed: 26 February 2022] Available at: https://www.nhsx.nhs.uk/media/documents/NHSX_AI_report.pdf

8. Joshi, I., Cushnan, D. 2020. A buyer's guide to AI in health and care. [Online] [Accessed: 26 February 2022] Available at: https://www.nhsx.nhs.uk/ai-lab/explore-all-resources/adopt-ai/a-buyers-guide-to-ai-in-health-and-care/

9. Lee, R., 2015. The law of the instrument. The Journal of Thoracic and Cardiovascular Surgery, 150(1), pp.167-168.

10. https://www.skinvision.com/

11. https://standardsdevelopment.bsigroup.com/projects/2021-00605#/section

12. https://digital.nhs.uk/data-and-information/information-standards/information-standards-and-data-collections-including-extractions/publications-and-notifications/standards-and-collections/dcb0129-clinical-risk-management-its-application-in-the-manufacture-of-health-it-systems

13. https://orchahealth.com/

14. Spatharou, A., Hieronimus, S., Jenkins, J. 2020. Transforming healthcare with AI: The impact on the workforce and organizations. [Online] [Accessed: 12 March 2022] Available at: https://www.mckinsey.com/industries/healthcare-systems-and-services/our-insights/transforming-healthcare-with-ai

15. https://theodi.org/article/the-data-ethics-canvas-2021/#1563365825519-a247d445-ab2d

16. https://ico.org.uk/for-organisations/guide-to-data-protection/key-dp-themes/explaining-decisions-made-with-artificial-intelligence/

17. Mol, D., Safi Harb, Y., Lobban, T.C., Riezebos, R.K., de Groot, J.R. and de Jong, J.S., 2018. Optimizing a Photophletysmography Algorithm for Atrial Fibrillation Detection Using Crowdsourcing Research Data. Circulation, 138(Suppl_1), pp.A15538-A15538.

18. https://www.tesco.com/data-portability/en-GB/

19. Jimenez,D. 2022. Profit for patients: can NFTs allow people to monetise their health data? [Online] [Accessed: 12 March 2022] Available at: https://www.pharmaceutical-technology.com/features/profit-patients-monetise-health-data-nfts/

Chapter 9

1. Strickland, E. 2022. Andrew Ng: Unbiggen AI The AI pioneer says it's time for smart-sized, "data-centric" solutions to big issues. [Online] [Accessed: 13 March 2022] Available at https://spectrum.ieee.org/andrew-ng-data-centric-ai

2. Chahal, H., Toner, H. 'Small Data' Are Also Crucial for Machine Learning. 2021. [Online] [Accessed: 13 March 2022] Available at https://www.scientificamerican.com/article/small-data-are-also-crucial-for-machine-learning/

3. Tucker, A., Wang, Z., Rotalinti, Y. and Myles, P., 2020. Generating high-fidelity synthetic patient data for assessing machine learning healthcare software. NPJ digital medicine, 3(1), pp.1-13.

4. Banner, N. 2020. A new approach to decisions about data. [Online] [Accessed: 27 March 2022] Available at: https://understandingpatientdata.org.uk/news/new-approach-decisions-about-data

5. Conrad, J., Knight, W. 2022. China Is About to Regulate AI—and the World Is Watching. [Online] [Accessed: 15 March 2022] Available at: https://www.wired.com/story/china-regulate-ai-world-watching/

6. Ada Lovelace Institute. 2022. Algorithmic impact assessment in healthcare. [Online] [Accessed: 14 March 2022] Available at https://www.adalovelaceinstitute.org/project/algorithmic-impact-assessment-healthcare/

7. https://www.gov.uk/government/publications/software-and-ai-as-a-medical-device-change-programme/software-and-ai-as-a-medical-device-change-programme

8. NHSX. 2022. The multi-agency advice service (MAAS). [Online] [Accessed: 12 February 2022] Available at: https://www.nhsx.nhs.uk/ai-lab/ai-lab-programmes/regulating-the-ai-ecosystem/the-multi-agency-advice-service-maas/

9. NHSX 2022. NCCID case study: Setting standards for testing Artificial Intelligence. [Online] [Accessed: 04 April 2022] Available at: https://www.nhsx.nhs.uk/ai-lab/explore-all-resources/develop-ai/nccid-case-study-setting-standards-for-testing-artificial-intelligence/

10. https://future.nhs.uk/DataAnalytics/grouphome

11. Miliard, M. 2021. Duke, Mayo Clinic, others launch innovative AI collaboration.[Online] [Accessed: 14 March 2022] Available at: https://www.healthcareitnews.com/news/duke-mayo-clinic-others-launch-innovative-ai-collaboration

12. Kerner, H. 2020. Too many AI researchers think real-world problems are not relevant. [Online] [Accessed: 14 March 2022] Available at: https://www.technologyreview.com/2020/08/18/1007196/ai-research-machine-learning-applications-problems-opinion/

13. Wagstaff, K., 2012. Machine learning that matters. arXiv preprint arXiv:1206.4656.

14. https://www.nhsx.nhs.uk/key-tools-and-info/procurement-frameworks/spark-dps-for-remote-monitoring/

15. Sheikh, A., Anderson, M., Albala, S., Casadei, B., Franklin, B.D., Richards, M., Taylor, D., Tibble, H. and Mossialos, E., 2021. Health information technology and digital innovation for national learning health and care systems. The Lancet Digital Health, 3(6), pp.e383-e396.

INDEX

Made in the USA
Las Vegas, NV
13 November 2023

80744424R00155